# The Technique and Practice of Psychoanalysis, Volume III: The Training Seminars of Ralph R. Greenson, M.D.

Monograph Series of the
Ralph R. Greenson Memorial Library of the
San Diego Psychoanalytic
Society and Institute

# The Technique and Practice of Psychoanalysis, Volume III: The Training Seminars of Ralph R. Greenson, M.D.

Transcripts of the Greenson Seminars on Assessment and the Initial Interviews

*Edited and Annotated by*

**Lee Jaffe**

International Universities Press, Inc.
Madison       Connecticut

Library of Congress Cataloging-in-Publication Data

The technique and practice of psychoanalysis, volume III, the training seminars of Ralph R. Greenson: transcripts of the Greenson seminars on assessment, and the initial interviews / edited and annotated by Lee Jaffe.
     p. cm.—(Monograph series of the Ralph R. Greenson Memorial Library of the San Diego Psychoanalytic Society and Institute; 3)
     Includes bibliographical references and index.
     ISBN 0-8236-6423-6
     1. Psychoanalysis. I. Greenson, Ralph R., 1911– II. Jaffe, Lee. III. Series.

RC504.T433 2004
616.89'17—dc21

2002032845

Manufactured in the United States of America

*Transcripts of*

# THE GREENSON SEMINARS

## on Assessment and the Initial Interviews

*TO ALL STUDENTS OF PSYCHOANALYSIS*

*AROUND THE WORLD—*

*CANDIDATES AND GRADUATES ALIKE*

# Table of Contents

# Acknowledgments

It would be impossible to thank individually all those who truly contributed to this book, in part because the list would have to begin with many of the people Ralph R. Greenson acknowledged over the years, his teachers, his patients, his students, and the Los Angeles Psychoanalytic Institute, where these seminars took place. Hildi Greenson deserves special thanks for her devotion to preserving her husband's work, which includes the archiving of these seminars, and for her generous efforts to continue to share his work.

I want to thank the Board of Directors and the Education Committee of the San Diego Psychoanalytic Society and Institute for encouraging me to do this project and for their ongoing support. They had the wisdom to suggest gently that this book would take longer than my original estimation, which was a comfort to me each time I had to put off work on it due to other responsibilities and commitments. I want to thank my mentors, who, as Ralph R. Greenson did for his students, helped me appreciate the deep understanding of humanity embodied in psychoanalytic perspectives. Also, I want to acknowledge my gratitude to Joyce Harding, then Administrator of the San Diego Psychoanalytic Society and Institute, for her indispensable efforts to organize and transform reams of very faded, barely readable transcripts of audiotapes into a legible, verbatim record of the seminars.

I am extremely grateful to Dr. Margaret Emery, Editor-in-Chief of International Universities Press for the suggestion that I not only organize and edit the seminars, but that I also annotate them to expand on the seminars and place Greenson's thoughts in a more contemporary framework. I am also appreciative for the careful readings of my first draft by Drs. Thomas Lian and Jaga Nath Glassman. My annotations are greatly improved by their astute feedback.

Finally, but most importantly, I want to thank my wife Susan, and my two daughters, Kate and Megan, for their continuing patience and support during the many hours I was working on this project. They are a daily reminder of what matters most in life.

# Introduction

In the pages that follow, the reader will "listen in" on Ralph R. Greenson's opening three introductory seminars on psychoanalytic technique, just as they took place in 1959 at the Los Angeles Psychoanalytic Institute. Dr. Greenson and his students will cover the important clinical subject of how to handle the initial contacts with a prospective patient. While some of Greenson's ideas about these preliminary matters of technique and clinical theory can be found in chapter 1 of the memorial Volume 2 of *The Technique and Practice of Psychoanalysis,* that chapter was unfinished at the time of Greenson's death in 1979, hence it was incomplete. Fortunately, these seminars offer a more complete account of Greenson's thoughts about clinical technique during the initial period of patient contact.

Greenson teaches with insight, wit, penetrating honesty, humility, humanity, and a deep sense of professional commitment. For me, the time spent editing and annotating these seminars has felt like time spent in Dr. Greenson's classroom. The more I "listened in," the more I found my-self simultaneously following three streams of thought. In one, I was learning about the technique of a master clini-cian. In the second, I was getting ideas about teaching by following Dr. Greenson working as an educator. His teach-ing style was highly organized but spontaneous, challenging but downright fun. Last but not least, I found myself in-spired by Greenson's passion for and dedication to his stu-dents, his patients, and psychoanalysis.

This volume has a history that goes back to 1985, when Hildi Greenson generously donated Ralph R. Greenson's professional library to the San Diego Psychoanalytic Insti-tute. Among the various papers and books donated were reams of verbatim transcripts of seminars he taught at the Los Angeles Psychoanalytic Institute. Even though the mim-eographed transcripts were barely legible, and despite the fact that they were not organized, the opportunity to reach back in time and sit in on seminars given by Ralph Greenson was irresistible. Hence the idea for this project took shape: the creation of a book that would allow the reader to experi-ence a masterful psychoanalytic teacher at work.

It became quickly apparent, however, that for several reasons the seminars would need to be edited. For one, conversation tends to be more wordy than written text. In the original transcripts, there were a number of times when Greenson wanted to emphasize certain points, so he re-peated them. Although I have not eliminated all the in-stances of such repetition, I have tried to make the seminars more lively to read by helping the material move more quickly from point to point. Also, there were places where the transcriber wrote that the voices on the audiotape were too soft to understand. Considering that these omissions occurred only when the students were speaking, it seems likely that the microphone for the tape recorder was located closer to Greenson than to the students. Nonetheless, in such instances where the students' dialogue was missing, it was necessary to read ahead to Greenson's responses and reconstruct their questions and comments. Fortunately, this did not occur frequently, and since it only occurred with the candidates' dialogue, all of Greenson's words are based on a verbatim record.

Transforming classroom recordings into a book required other editorial efforts as well. For example, I have provided formal references where possible, and I have created a formal, detailed table of contents rather than an index. Fortunately, Greenson was a highly organized teacher with a clear lesson plan. As a result, it was relatively easy to divide the seminars into sections similar to the outline system that Greenson used in his classic book on psychoanalytic technique. One look at the table of contents will convey the degree to which his teaching followed a detailed lesson plan.

In order to facilitate the interplay between the seminars and the annotations, this book is designed so the reader can follow both without having to turn pages back and forth. For that reason, the edited transcripts of the seminars are on the right-hand pages of the book, whereas the left-hand pages are reserved for annotations. Where necessary, some of the more lengthy annotations are continued at the bottom of the right-hand pages in order to preserve this format. There are several reasons for the annotations. In some places, they are an effort to provide clarification, detail, and more background information. In other places, the annotations are there to stimulate thought as to how Greenson's ideas in the 1950s are relevant to clinical practice in the twenty-first century. For example, how might Greenson's ideas inform the contemporary practice of psychotherapy in the managed care setting? In the annotations I offer examples of how managed care providers can improve their skills by finding ways to integrate the clinical wisdom of psychoanalysts like Ralph Greenson into their practices, whether they are providing psychotropic medications, psychotherapy, or both.

Greenson practiced psychoanalysis at a time when doctors made the decisions about treatment plans. Today, many of these decisions are governed by the policies of managed care companies. During Greenson's time, insurance companies regularly reimbursed patients for intensive, insight-oriented psychological treatments, psychoanalysts were at the

center of medical school psychiatric training programs, and
the American Psychiatric Association's diagnostic manual
relied on psychodynamic concepts. Psychoanalytic ideas
were prominent in the field of psychology. Nonetheless,
considerations of how best to respond to referral sources
still apply, when a patient is referred for an evaluation or
for psychotherapy. No matter who is the source of the referral, the psychoanalyst may decide analysis is the treatment
of choice. For this reason, it is important to handle the
referral process in a manner that fosters the potential for
analytic treatment. Also, since insurance benefits rarely pay
for psychoanalysis any more, patients often wish to begin
with a less expensive, less time-consuming attempt at psychotherapy. A trial of psychotherapy may be undertaken, with
the analyst indicating that it may be necessary to convert to
analysis in order to have an effective treatment. Much of this
has changed, and yet Greenson's teachings are as important
today as they were fifty some years ago. In some ways, the
issues he takes up are more important today. For example,
he and his students struggle with how to advocate for the
patient, which is a problem facing many clinicians in the
managed care environment. They take up the question of
how to arrive at a meaningful diagnosis that points the way
to an effective treatment. They look at the reasons for need-
ing informed consent, and the crucial issue of confidentiality, a sine qua non of psychotherapy, which has been
challenged by contemporary efforts to have records easily
available for authorization review. In the end, Greenson
presents us with a model of how to practice and how to
teach that is filled with both passion and precision.

# 1

# Introduction to the Preliminary Interviews

## Opening Remarks

*Greenson:* Let me tell you a little about this seminar on psychoanalytic technique. The first subject we are going to discuss will be the preliminary interviews. I intend to discuss this subject with you until we have covered all phases of the subject. By *preliminary interviews* I mean those interviews which take place between the patient and the analyst until the analyst decides whether this patient should be analyzed, which then ushers in the next round of interviews, which I call the "Transitional Interviews." So I divide the two interview categories under the heading "The Beginning of Analysis." The section on preliminary interviews is divided into initial interviews or the opening phase of the preliminary interviews, followed by the closing phase of the preliminary interviews.

I want to say there is no rush, we can take two years to do this whole discussion, so let's do it well and thoroughly

1

[1] Here Greenson is juxtaposing one therapist's inclination to assess psychopathology to another's emphasis on protecting the patient's access to psychoanalytic treatment. For contemporary clinicians, how these concerns play out will vary depending on their diagnostic framework. The DSM-IV (American Psychiatric Association, 1994), for example, largely bases diagnosis on descriptive criteria like duration of symptoms or number of specified symptoms. Ascertaining such a diagnosis requires questioning the patient according to the criteria for a given DSM-IV diagnosis. On the other hand, a psychoanalytic diagnosis is based on structural criteria linked to ego functioning, like the capacity to utilize affects as signals that summon adaptive responses. Otto Kernberg has elaborated a complex schema for such structural diagnoses (1984). In his system, the term *borderline* refers to a number of formal aspects of psychological functioning (e.g., perceptions are highly vulnerable to being shaped by affects) that can be manifest in various character types. This is quite different from the DSM-IV use of the term *borderline* that defines a specific character type, the infantile personality, which requires five or more of the nine descriptors listed in the diagnostic handbook. Given that these issues are so relevant to the pages that follow, several issues related to diagnostic considerations are relevant.

For one, it is interesting to note that there is a parallel between Greenson's comments here about analysts' concerns in the initial interviews with detecting psychosis, and current-day concerns with detecting borderline ego pathology. The style of initial interview that Otto Kernberg suggests, for example, with his "structural interview," raises controversies similar to the issues Greenson is addressing. Kernberg's structural interview involves systematic challenges to the patient's inner resources as a way of exposing ego weaknesses or regressive vulnerabilities. For more information see Kernberg's chapter on the structural interview (1984).

Another consideration here is the role of psychological testing in the initial assessment of the patient for analysis. It is possible to make a referral for testing in order to answer the question about a possible psychosis, and at the same time protect the transference situation. In my experience, however, there is a range of opinion concerning the usefulness of psychological testing in treatment planning from never needed to frequently requested. In 1967, Greenson commented that psychological testing can help with the diagnosis, but might produce disturbing side effects (p. 52). In an incomplete work that appeared posthumously, Greenson remarked that he regretted never being trained in the discipline of psychological testing, which he noted was a useful diagnostic tool (1979, p. 25). The usefulness of psychological testing led Kernberg (1975, p. 25) to comment that the detection of primary process thinking through the use of projective tests makes sophisticated psychological testing an indispensable instrument for the structural, psychoanalytic diagnosis of borderline personality disorder and for effective treatment planning. Kernberg refers to "sophisticated" psychological testing rather than just "psychological testing," because he is referring to a special approach to psychological testing that is guided by the principles of psychoanalytic theory. For a more careful and ask all the questions. What I would like to start with is the opening phase of the preliminary interviews, but before we actually start talking about the patient, let me start the ball rolling by making a few remarks. There is nothing sacred about what I say, so you may interrupt me any time you feel you have something to say or to ask. Please don't hesitate.

First of all, some outstanding points about the preliminary interviews. There is more variation of how the preliminary interviews are carried out by psychoanalysts than any other phase of analysis. You can get considerable agreement on how you handle resistance, how you handle acting out, how you handle transference, and how you handle termination, but about initial interviews there is a greater diversity than about any other phase of analysis; it's very interesting. I think this is because analysts vary greatly in what they consider to be the important things to look for in the initial interviews and in what they consider to be the greatest dangers in the initial interviews. Some analysts who are more psychiatrically oriented or trained have a greater awareness that in the initial interviews, one of the important things is to detect psychosis. The aim of detecting psychosis governs the way they handle the initial interviews. Other analysts who have little psychiatric training, or who didn't like psychiatric training, or who do not care to be allied with psychiatrists, are much more aware of the fact that in the initial interviews you had better be careful or you'll contaminate the transference and spoil the transference situation later on.[1]

---

consideration of the methods and uses of a psychoanalytic approach to psychological testing in the diagnostic process there are a number of resources including but not limited to the following: Rapaport, Gill, and Schafer (1945–1946); Schafer (1954, 1967); Kwawer, Lerner, Lerner, and Sugarman (1980); Kissen (1986); Lerner (1991). Greenson recognized that this was a unique form of "psychoanalytic" psychological testing that requires specialized training when he commented that "it was often difficult to find a competent psychological tester" (1979, p. 25). Stephen Appelbaum (1977) notes in the Menninger Foundation Report the finding that sophisticated psychological testing was the most penetrating, accurate diagnostic assessment tool. This finding was the result of an extensive research project.

[2] This candidate's comment about how to handle the referring analyst needs to be understood in terms of the 1950s. It was a time when psychoanalysis was a much more prevalent, popular form of treatment than it is today and direct referrals for psychoanalysis were commonplace. Since then, managed care has dramatically changed insurance benefits, making it more difficult to build a psychoanalytic practice in many places. Insurance rarely covers psychoanalysis as a benefit, and the managed care companies often control the referral networks. Direct referrals for analysis are far less prevalent in the early twenty-first century than in the 1950s. When Greenson was teaching, the original *Diagnostic and Statistical Manual* (DSM) of the American Psychiatric Association and the DSM-II that followed had a number of diagnostic criteria for psychiatric disorders based on psychodynamic concepts. Since that time, with the changes in the DSM-III and even more so with the DSM-IV, American psychiatry has shifted from a psychoanalytic, dynamic point of view to a descriptive point of view that no longer differentiates between manifest symptoms and their underlying, unconscious causes.

Nonetheless, the comments that follow about how much to know about the patient before beginning an analysis are relevant to understanding the process of converting a patient from psychotherapy to analysis, although the context is different from learning information from a referral source. Thus, the reader can read these passages with the added idea of clarifying how conversion differs from the situation of a new referral (i.e., the knowledge the analyst has from doing psychotherapy with the patient prior to the conversion to analysis).

*Candidate:* I am having a little trouble following you. I don't know if the others are, but we have skipped a step, and that is how you handle the referring analyst.[2] How much you listen to, and how much you don't. Let's say that I don't want to hear a thing about so-and-so. I want to wait to form my own opinion.

*Greenson:* That's interesting. It would never have occurred to me that it could be a problem, but now that you mention it: How much should you listen or not listen to the referring analyst or whoever refers the patient? Does it matter whether it's an analyst? Before I start to talk about the technique of the initial interviews, I'll talk about how you handle the interaction with the source of the referral.

*Candidate:* Another problem that might be brought up in terms of the initial interview concerns the conscious and unconscious predispositions of the analyst. The question of whether or not the analyst should take a particular patient.

*Greenson:* This is another point I'll make a note of and talk about before I talk about technique, but I don't want to bring it in now. Also, I think just as we could talk about the referral we could also talk about the patient's first telephone call. I don't want to start with the first telephone call either, even though it is important chronologically. I think if I get across to you some basic principles about the initial interview, some of these other concerns will be a little easier for you, and they won't require a great deal of explicit detail.

At the outset, I want to make two general points. First, analysts differ in whether to stress the detection of psychosis or whether to stress the danger of spoiling the transference situation. These differences influence them in how they conduct initial interviews. Second, conducting initial interviews is a skill that is very different from psychoanalytic skill. I think you've got to face it, there are many analysts who are great sitting behind the patient, but are lousy sitting in front of the patient. It's a completely different kind of skill.

[3] Elsewhere, Greenson (1979, pp. 14–20) makes a number of comments relevant to the initial interview that expand on his comments here. He raises issues such as the atmosphere of the office, the patient who wants to keep treatment a secret, the shame in being a patient, the home office, and soundproofing. In other words, he addresses a number of issues that will influence the initial interview, and that are therefore important to keep in mind. For example, where the office is concerned he describes creating a "working area that is private, comfortable, and aesthetically pleasing" (p. 18). In the true spirit of the psychoanalytic approach, Greenson respects the fact that how a patient presents in the initial interview will be influenced by anything and everything that the patient encounters in that first meeting, in addition to the interviewer's approach.

Nowadays, there are additional requirements of the initial interviews. For many clinicians, their individual discipline and their local laws require that the patient give informed consent to the evaluative process and treatment recommendations. Also, there are limitations to confidentiality (e.g., child abuse), which the patient will in all likelihood not know about. Therapists must decide how to explain the privileges and limitations of confidentiality during these initial meetings. Will it be done the same way every time, in a formulaic manner, or is it better to customize these requirements to fit the needs of the individual patient? Whatever a clinician decides, Greenson is saying that it is important to appreciate that all aspects of the initial interviews will influence the way the patient presents in these early meetings. In order to arrive at an accurate assessment of the patient, the interviewer must assess the patient's reactions to the legal and ethical issues as they are explained. For example, does the patient who learns of limitations to confidentiality shut down, and why? Does the patient who is informed about treatment ask questions, do they really understand, or do they pretend to understand while they passively put themselves in the hands of the therapist? These are but a few of the diagnostic considerations that are raised when the impact of all aspects of therapist–patient interaction are appreciated.

[4] By nonanalytic therapies Greenson is differentiating descriptive psychiatric approaches that cure by providing medications or advice from the dynamic, analytic approaches that seek to cure by uncovering repressed, unconscious sources of conflict. He will go on in the next section to elaborate on these differences. At the same time he is indirectly raising the question about how much to define psychoanalysis by the use of the couch, which has gotten more attention in recent years (Moraitis, 1995; Ross, 1999).

What exactly is the skill of the face-to-face situation as compared to the patient lying down with you sitting behind them? I think it will become clearer when we talk about the technique or special problems of the initial interviews, but I do want to make the statement that the skill of conducting initial interviews is very different from conducting an analysis. I have seen candidates with no psychoanalytic training at all who can conduct the initial interviews with tact and finesse. I have seen analysts who have worked many, many years, who were training analysts, but who were poor at conducting initial interviews. So poor were they in some cases that the patients ran away and would never come back, and from what the patients told me about how the initial interview was conducted, I didn't blame them.[3] It's such a different skill. It requires such different things of you that I think it's worth paying a little attention to. It's such a different way of establishing a relationship with a person. This is not strange to you, is it? I think you yourself have seen it and know it.

*Candidate:* Yes, the face-to-face situation in the initial interview is the way we work in psychotherapy as opposed to psychoanalysis.

*Greenson:* Yes, but the initial interview situation is much more allied to the nonanalytic than the analytic therapies, although both have to do with strictly face-to-face situations.[4] We have to recognize that sitting up in front of the patient, letting yourself be seen by a patient poses special problems and makes special demands, different than when you sit behind a patient and are not seen. All right, so all of that is a kind of introduction to the problem of the preliminary interviews and particularly the opening phase or the initial interviews, and if there are no questions about these particular general remarks, let me go on to a few historical remarks, just briefly.

[5] At the time of these lectures, the American Psychiatric Association's psychiatric diagnostic system (DSM-II [1968]) had incorporated a more psychodynamic framework than in the "preanalytic" days. Since that time, however, psychiatry has returned to the kind of descriptive, fact-finding diagnostic approach that Greenson is discussing. The notion that the DSM-IV (1994) is an improvement in earlier editions because psychodynamic criteria have been replaced with more "objective," observable descriptive criteria is in fact a return to a former system rather than a new one. Since nomothetic and idiographic aspects of a psychodiagnosis are both important to achieving a penetrating understanding of a patient, taking one or the other as more correct misses the need for both.

## Historical Remarks

*Greenson:* I think it's important to remember that before psychoanalysis really made its impact in psychiatry, the initial interviews were essentially a battery of questions, fact-finding, a search for neurotic stigmata, signs, symptoms, a cross-examination of the patient in which your aim was, "goddammit, what's wrong with this patient!" and you determined this by asking the patient questions and getting answers. The whole emphasis in the preanalytic days was, if I get enough facts from the patient, I'll find out what's wrong with him.[5] It was fact finding. It was diagnosis hunting. It was a cross-examination. You asked a series of questions, usually in the same order, and you usually wrote on a form and you filled in the blanks. You focused on filling in the blanks. Above all, there was no recognition of the importance of your participation in these initial interviews. You were the observer, you were the recorder, you were the diagnostician. Now I said, incidentally, that this was in the preanalytic days, but I must correct myself because it's not true.

I'll tell you a story. About six months ago an orthopedist called me and said would I please see a patient. I know this man a long time so he has learned by now not to call me for this, since I usually say, well, gee, I'd love to, but I don't have the time. But he said please do me a favor. He said, she's so antipsychiatry that he's got to get her to see someone because it's a case which involves a lot of money, it's a legal case that involves a trial, and he must get a psychiatric opinion. I said, well, since you make such an issue, all right, if she can wait, I'll see her. I gave him a time a few weeks hence and this woman came. She came, incidentally, on crutches, hobbling, and it was raining, so it was more than six months ago because it was in the last rainy season.

She sat down with a smile on her face, I helped her to be comfortable, and I said: Well, doctor so-and-so said I should see you, he told me very little about you, only that you had some injury or some accident and that you now needed a psychiatric opinion about your situation. That's

all I really do know. She said, Well, oh I had quite an accident, and she launched into telling me the story of her accident, and I listened. I asked a few leading questions and when she paused, she poured out a whole megillah about the accident. It was very interesting, very interesting, because it started out that she had this accident with her husband and although she was injured in the car he wasn't. Since then she has been paralyzed and can't walk; not only paralyzed and can't walk, but she also can't control her bladder, so she has a catheter in her now. While she was sitting there, talking, she said I have a catheter, and it collects the urine in me.

It was really amazing, sounded like a real old-fashioned hysterical kind of paralysis. I hadn't seen one of these in years. I must have shown my surprise when she told me about the accident as I said, my god, your husband was with you and he wasn't hurt. She said, yes, and *now* he's taking care of me. I said, *now* he's taking care of you. Yes, she said, you know I used to be a nurse, and you know how I met my husband? I said, no. She said, I met my husband when he was in the hospital and he was having a leg amputated. I helped him get well, and you know, incidentally, he couldn't urinate either and I had to catheterize him. I thought, oh brother, this is a juicy case, look how nice, her husband couldn't urinate, now she can't urinate.

After some forty minutes I said, incidentally, the orthopedist said you hated psychiatrists. She said, I do, I do. I said, oh, I don't notice your hating me. She said well, you're not like the rest of them. I said I don't understand. She said, you're not writing notes, you're looking at me. So I looked at her sort of quizzically and she said: Well, you know, they sent me to a psychiatrist. I went to see this man, he sat me down, he took out a form and he began to ask me questions. He never once looked at me, he just filled in the form. I felt that man hated me, he only loved his form, he didn't give a goddam for me. After he asked me some questions, about a half an hour, I got up and walked out.

[6] It seems that in 1959 Greenson did not suspect that psychiatry in the 1990s would once again embrace this preanalytic, diagnostic attitude in the form of the DSM-IV. Greenson is clearly wanting to highlight an important danger associated with a descriptive approach to psychodiagnosis if one views the patient as a means to get at information rather than viewing the patient as a person who is entering into a new relationship. It is interesting to note that at the same time psychoanalysts have increasingly appreciated the importance of individual relationships, especially childhood relationships, the return to descriptive diagnosis in psychiatry has made it easier for the managed care movement to mechanize the diagnostic process, making it less and less individualized. The importance of the "relationship" as a source of cure is deemphasized or lost entirely. Also, the mental status examination, which depends on observations of the patient, is at risk for becoming a lost art. It is very difficult to observe a patient's thought processes or facial expression with closed-ended questions that are asked while filling out forms. The challenge here is to find creative ways to meet the requirements of managed care.

Clearly, the descriptive approach to diagnosis is preferred by the managed care system. When economic concerns are foremost, an approach that emphasizes the need for a meaningful relationship with the patient is undesirable. It takes time to form relationships, and the psychotherapist's time is money. For this reason, and not for reasons of treatment outcome, psychoanalysis is not suited to the managed are approach. One hazard in the managed care approach is to mistakenly assume that the knowledge gathered is complete, and the importance of the relationship is secondary to other considerations. While a medication may alleviate a symptom, compliance with the prescription may rely more on the quality of the doctor–patient relationship.

The establishment of a relationship is limited by the managed care system often requiring that the patient be diagnosed quickly and an efficient treatment begun at once. Descriptive assessments are often made on the basis of questionnaires more than time spent with the patient. From Greenson's perspective, however, no matter what the treatment approach, including medications, the need to establish a caring relationship is crucial. David Rapaport appreciated this problem when he devised a psychoanalytic system for psychological testing, in that his system required the examiner to memorize all the test materials, so that the focus could be on the person being examined and not on the test materials (Rapaport, Gill, and Schafer, 1945–1946).

I must say I thought she was right. I was shocked. So when I say, this was in preanalytic days when they used to do a battery of questions with the patient and just recorded facts, and then on the basis of the facts you tried to make a diagnosis, I'm wrong. This is a preanalytic attitude, but it's not historically or temporally preanalytic, because you still see it today.[6] So that's one segment in the history of the initial interview. The other interesting thing to notice is that in the early analytic days, the neglect of the initial interview is amazing. Freud has one sentence on the initial interview

Despite the fundamental differences between these two systems, Greenson's ideas can inform and improve the diagnostic, psychopharmacologic, and the psychotherapeutic work done within the managed care system. For example, if it is necessary to get forms filled out, patients might be asked to fill out and return forms before coming to the office, so they are greeted upon arrival with a focus on establishing a relationship, not on forms and descriptive fact finding. If there is a concern that filling out forms in advance could have a negative impact on the patient and the initial interview, it should be possible to give the forms at the end of the initial interview and ask that they be returned. This has the advantage of establishing some assessment alliance with the patient before the forms are completed.

[7]Although Freud did not refer to the initial interviews in other places, it is instructive to have a more complete account of Freud's comments in this reference to the Dora case (1905). As Greenson notes, Freud starts by saying:

> I begin the treatment, indeed, by asking the patient to give the whole story of his life and illness, but even so the information I receive is never enough to let me see my way about the case. This first account may be compared to an unnavigable river whose stream is at one moment choked by masses of rock and at another divided and lost among shallows and sandbanks. I cannot help wondering how it is that the authorities can produce such smooth and precise histories in cases of hysteria. As a matter of fact the patients are incapable of giving such reports about themselves. They can, indeed, give the physician plenty of coherent information about this or that period of their lives; but it is sure to be followed by another period as to which their communications run dry, leaving gaps unfilled, and riddles unanswered, and then again will come yet another period which will remain totally obscure and unilluminated by even a single piece of information [p. 16].

Here Freud is being true to his science of the unconscious. He is asserting his belief that patients cannot tell their entire life stories due to repression. He does not expect that patients will be able to reveal the underlying reasons for the illness they suffer. Freud expects that these aspects of the history will be omitted, underemphasized, or altered. In these lectures, however, Greenson is not looking for the initial interviews to tell the patient's story in a manner that will expose the underlying causes and reasons for the illness; this is the work of the analysis. For Greenson, the initial interviews are conducted in order to determine if the patient is capable of doing the work of the analysis, and to determine if the patient's difficulties are of a sort that analysis can treat.

[8] The term *anamnesis* in Deutsch (1939) refers to the collected data concerning a patient. In his paper, Deutsch describes a technique he teaches students so they can interview patients with psychosomatic symptoms and get at the underlying psychic structure that produces the psychosomatic symptoms. It is an interesting method. He suggests letting patients go over their "physical" problems until they have no more to say, after which the interviewer merely restates one of the patient's more recent statements with an interrogative tone. At this point, Deutsch claims that left alone, patients often produce more information that begins to include information about relationships and traumas, which permits the interviewer to develop insights about the underlying

in all his writings, and that's in the Dora case,[7] where he says that he asks the patient in the beginning to tell the whole story of their life and troubles. That's all. Then he goes on to say, I know they can't. Freud mentioned one sentence. Fenichel has nothing about it. Glover, who writes a lot about the opening phase, so-called, completely disregards the initial interviews. Ella Freeman-Sharpe says: "Well in the first hour I try to arrange matters of time and fee and some practical things and get the patient as quickly as possible onto the couch, by the latest the second interview."

I think the first important analyst who made a contribution to the initial interview was Felix Deutsch. He wrote a paper on associative anamnesis which I think is a real classical paper in terms of one aspect of initial interviews and how to conduct them.[8]

structure of the psychosomatic illness. As Greenson notes, it is a classic paper, albeit I suspect one that is rarely read nowadays (I had not heard of it before editing these lectures). It describes a technique of interviewing that facilitates a process whereby patients reveal themselves, rather than one where patients go through a series of decision trees based on descriptive, diagnostic categories.

[9] In the two works (1937, 1948), Reik described his belief that it was crucial for the analysts to pay attention to their own reactions as well as their patients' productions. He felt it was possible to listen to find "hidden" connections by listening inwards not just outwards, which clearly has relevance for the initial interviews. For example, in *Listening with the Third Ear* (1948), Reik describes an initial interview as follows: "While I listened to the patient's report, I felt some hidden emotional connections. It was as if out of his tale some cues emerged, some elusive lights appeared here and there. The initial cloudiness of his situation seemed to recede in a few spots. It was obvious that the man became ill when a wish that he had nursed for a long time became a reality."

[10] Robert Knight wrote seminal articles about psychodiagnosis and diagnostic categories. For example, in his article (1953) on "Borderline States," Knight takes up the issue of how to assess for those conditions, that seem neither to meet clear criteria for neurotic nor for psychotic diagnoses. Clearly, Greenson thinks of Knight here because of the effort to help the clinician with certain diagnostic challenges at the point of the initial interviews.

[11] Probably the work Greenson has in mind here is Merton Gill's article "Ego Psychology and Psychotherapy" (1951). Here, Gill addresses which kinds of treatments are appropriate for different problems, he describes the techniques of various treatment modalities, and then he goes on to talk about the limitations of those treatments. In other words, Gill deals with the very business of initial interviews, which is the determination of treatment recommendations, if any are appropriate, and the preparation of the patient for those recommendations. Greenson probably is also referring to Gill's later article in which he compares the indications and goals of psychoanalysis with exploratory psychotherapy (1954). Again, in this article, Gill takes up indications for different treatment approaches, but as compared with the others Greenson mentions here, Gill takes up these questions in a comprehensive and systematic way.

The first group of analysts who gave any importance at all to the initial interview, is the Washington School, particularly under the leadership of Harry Stack Sullivan, but up until 1940 the analysts more or less neglected it. Then you could read people like Reik in *Surprise and the Psychoanalyst*, and later on in *Listening with the Third Ear* which came out much later.[9] Reik made certain remarks about initial interviews in which he showed somewhat unsystematically how one could use one's skills, but otherwise, it was a total loss until Knight[10] and then Gill[11]; Gill's work I think is the most systematic and the most interesting to read, although it's again geared to the psychiatric interview, but the basic principles are the same.

*Candidate:* So was there no attention given to initial interviews early on in analytic seminars?

*Greenson:* No time was spent on it. We never had discussions of initial interviews, never. In fact I remember when I was working for the draft board, you know in 1941, 1942, when they started draft boards. I remember one time we had a seminar and I presented our hair-raising experiences in interviewing draftees. The whole psychoanalytic group came to listen to us and said how did you do it, how did you conduct interviews where you had one or two minutes per interview? They were fascinated that you could do it. Just fascinated that you could in a minute or two make a decision whether a guy was draftable or not. We had a whole evening on how we interviewed these draftees in roughly one minute. Complicated cases took two or three minutes.

Patients were all naked lined up outside the door, we sat about the distance from that door. They had a sheet of paper and they walked in naked, about 400 men. Then, you watched them walk. What did they do with the sheet of paper? Like some guys put it down on their seat. This was part of it: They had that damned sheet of paper, they were naked, there was a whole bunch of guys, so we watched how they walked over to us. Then, we had time to ask two or

[12] Greenson prioritizes three diagnostic screening questions here, and while he does not explain the reasoning behind these three particular questions, they were linked to the diagnostic task at hand, which was to assess psychological suitability to enter the Army. Given such limited time, Greenson went directly to basic regulatory functions, with the understandable inclusion of sexual functioning. If he noted any irregularities in the answers to these three questions, he would pursue them further.

This section does point out how the initial interviews can be of varying length, depending on how much information is needed to answer the questions at hand. If all you can offer a patient is medications or brief psychotherapy, you do not need all the information required to determine if he or she is a good candidate for more in-depth, exploratory psychotherapy or psychoanalysis. Taken to its absurd extreme, there is no need for an initial interview if you cannot offer the patient any treatment at all.

[13] In asserting the idea that training analysts "took advantage of the fact" that their candidate patients were psychiatrists in making their initial assessments, Greenson is suggesting that the achievement of becoming a psychiatrist provides essential information to the psychiatrist–training analyst who is assessing the potential candidate for analyzability. Today, this could refer to the idea that the analyst who interviews the potential analytic candidate who is a psychiatrist, psychologist, or social worker and who is in analytic training, is unlikely to go over issues of informed consent, knowing that the patient is already well informed. As a result, therapists often miss aspects of the initial interview in their own treatment that they will need to include in the treatment of most of their own patients. What Greenson meant exactly is unclear. Perhaps he refers to qualities that a psychiatrist was assumed to possess; intelligence, for example. Maybe he refers to the idea that psychiatrist-patients come in and spontaneously give more of the needed information, making the training analyst's job easier. The point here is that psychoanalysts-in-training may not get firsthand experience of the initial interview process as the beginning of their own training analyses.

Whatever Greenson has in mind, several contemporary issues are relevant here. For one, it is important to be leery of assumptions about suitability for psychoanalytic training based on a potential student's professional achievements in psychiatry, especially given the current biological trend in psychiatry training programs. The hazard here is that a useful familiarity becomes a substitute for a thorough initial evaluation. Moreover, even the familiarity is less likely nowadays because there is a clear trend in the United States toward training analysts who come from fields other than psychiatry, like psychology and social work. Does that make such candidates less known to the training analyst who is a psychiatrist? Without hearing Greenson's tone of voice, it is unclear whether or not he may be subtly critical here, commenting that the training analyst may rely on criteria that speak more to a countertransference reaction in the broad sense, than relying on an astute evaluation method. In many ways, this comment raises more questions than it answers, but it makes clear the need to be wary of assumptions, both conscious and unconscious.

three questions. My first question was always the same: "How do you sleep?" Basic question. I think if I had to ask one question of a person and that's all, I would ask: "How do you sleep?" Then next was, of course: "How do you eat?" And the third was: "Do you get laid?" Based on their answers to those three questions, they were either in the Army, or you had a problem which took a little longer time.[12]

But, as I said, there was no seminar on the initial interviews. That was considered more or less psychiatric in the days when I was a candidate, and I think to this day, you have never had a seminar really in which one discussed at any length the initial interviews. It's gone over rather briefly. It's taken for granted you know how to do it. If I were to ask you, how did your own analyst do it, I know that he takes advantage of the fact that you're psychiatrists, that's how he does it.[13]

*Candidate:* Not doing much initial interview face-to-face also has to do with not wanting to have preconceptions about the patient prior to the analysis.

*Greenson:* Yes, but it also has to do with the anxiety about facing the patient, don't kid yourself about it. Don't hide behind the idea that this has to do only with preconceptions, I don't agree with that at all, it has to do with prejudices and anxieties as well. I don't care what the patient was, I don't care what your preconception was, I don't care if a patient was sent to me by Sigmund Freud with a letter saying this man should be analyzed. I would want to take my own sweet time coming to my conclusion, what I thought ought to be done with this patient, and not plunk him down on the couch because old Siggy said so. I wonder what kind of respect that patient would have for me, and how that would interfere with the later transference, if all I did was say, if he said you should be analyzed, then let's begin. Please, never do that. If I ever send you a patient and say this man should be analyzed, you make up your own mind, don't you take my word for it.

[14] This section deals with a topic of great significance given the increased demand for information brought on by the managed care movement and current controversies in trend-setting agencies like the U.S. Department of Health and Human Resources that governs Medicare. There is also great relevance here to medical–legal work. More and more, psychotherapists and psychoanalysts are being asked to make the psychotherapeutic setting open to the scrutiny of third parties, who may or may not possess the needed training in order to understand the information. Often, either the patient or the therapist-analyst is forced to disclose confidential information or the insurance benefits are denied.

The increased computerization of records threatens to make highly confidential treatment information easily accessible, without requiring the patient's explicit authorization each time the records are seen by a third party. Confidentiality, which is viewed by most psychotherapists and psychoanalysts as a sine qua non for effective treatment, is currently under siege. How each therapist-analyst deals with this dilemma will vary, but Greenson provides a very important guideline for making such decisions. He reminds us that we are trained first and foremost to protect the patient's best interests. All other considerations should be subordinated to acting in the best interests of the patient.

# 2

# Do You Take Notes During the Initial Interview?[14]

*Candidate:* Do you make it a practice never to write anything down during these interviews or do you take notes during the initial interview?

*Greenson:* I don't write anything down in the initial interview. Nothing. We'll talk about note taking later on, but let me say I don't find it necessary to write anything down. If I have to fill out a form for the insurance or something, I do it at the end of the interview, and I'll tell the patient, listen, we have to stop now, let me write down a few things, please tell me, what's your name, address, etc. But I make it distinctly something I do when I'm through with the work of the interview. Then I will say, all right, let's take care of some paperwork. Otherwise, nothing.

[15] Since Greenson gave lectures in 1959, professional developments in psychiatry, psychology, and social work, changes brought about by managed care, and changes in state and federal laws (e.g., Medicare), have placed more requirements on psychotherapists to keep notes and have specified what must be covered in the content of those notes. Today, it is not a question of whether or not to keep notes, but what to include in the notes.

[16] This is a reference to the tormented writer, Rainer Maria Rilke, who lived during Freud's time, and who was also a friend of Lou Andreas-Salomé. Rilke, in the fourth of his *Duino Elegies*, writes about the dividedness of human consciousness in a manner that poetically captures the essence of neurotic suffering. Greenson refers to Rilke as an example of someone who was brilliant but endured great neurotic unhappiness.

## Are You Legally Required to Take Notes?

*Candidate:* Just one other point about the notes. I don't generally do this, but I have never really asked. Is it a legal requirement for doctors to make a note or two about the patient? I have often worried about this. Is it necessary to keep notes from the initial contact with the patient?

*Greenson:* I don't know if there's something legal about it.[15]

*Candidate:* They always say doctors should keep records.

*Greenson:* You should keep records, yes, and they may insist that you keep some. I usually keep some records. When I get home of an evening, if I had a new patient that day, I'll take a sheet of paper and I'll write down something like Joe Berkowitz (fictional name), age 25, referred from Stockbridge, artistic looking, Rilke-like figure,[16] studying drama, gets straight A's in school, and hates himself for it. Wants to be artist, schizoid, two years of psychotherapy in Stockbridge, one year psychotherapy Berkeley, now willing to try straight analysis??? Schizzy? Referred to . . . and so on.

*Candidate:* I think it's a good idea not to have referral notes from a single meeting, because I once had some records subpoenaed, and I was glad I didn't have certain information. I only saw this woman once. She was upset because she'd been having an extramarital relationship with a doctor that I knew very well, and the husband didn't know about it. If this had been in the notes, he would have found out in court about it.

## What if Your Notes Are Requested by a Subpoena?

*Greenson:* But I think you have no right to have anybody subpoena your notes.

*Candidate:* You mean the court does not have the right. What is the law?

[17] Putting Greenson's obvious passion for his patients' better interest aside for a moment, there are ways to protect your patients and respond to the law. For example, when a subpoena arrives, contact the patient and try to obtain a release. If the patient refuses, discuss the issue, and see if it can be worked out therapeutically. It is a rare case that cannot be solved in this manner, respecting both your patient and the law.

[18] This was a case where Roy Grinker, Sr., was told he had to turn over his clinical notes in the trial of a man for murder. It was the prosecution's hope that the notes would help convict the man on trial. Grinker refused the court's demand and faced the threat of going to jail, but in the end his decision to refuse to release the records was upheld by the courts (Personal communication, Robert Galatzer-Levy, 1998).

*Greenson:* To hell with the law—you owe something to your patient. It's not a point about the law. I don't think the law has any right to subpoena your notes. I think you could go up to the Supreme Court and they wouldn't get you to give up your notes.[17]

*Candidate:* There was the Grinker case in Chicago.[18]

*Greenson:* What about the Grinker case?

*Candidate:* He refused.

*Greenson:* And what happened to him?

*Candidate:* He won.

*Greenson:* Of course he won.

*Candidate:* Why leave yourself wide open for this. I have made it a practice that I take absolutely no notes.

## What Is the Best Protection from Legal Liability?

*Greenson:* Gentlemen, stop quibbling with yourselves, and stop beating around the bush. You do what's best for the patient, goddammit, you're not lawyers! For the patient's sake don't take notes. Listen to him. Observe him. React to him. Not for the lawyers, and not for the Supreme Court. And if it helps you with your patient to take notes, please take notes, even if you have to go to jail to hide them, take them, but if it doesn't help your patient and interferes with the patient, don't take notes. I want to say this, I know I'm saying it with great feeling, but I feel that way about it. You're therapists, not wise guys out beating the lawyers! The only way you can beat lawyers is in one way, you're interested in your patient, not in the fee, or the jury. You don't have a chance against a smart lawyer if you want to outsmart them. You can only outsmart one by being more honest, that will stop them every time. But enough of this. I don't want to go on with this.

[19] Here Greenson gives us his bottom line attitude about note taking. He wants his patients to feel they have his undivided attention, and he wants his patients to realize that he is there for their benefit. Consider the patient whose first office contact is with someone who gathers information about insurance coverage. Will the patient feel this is treatment for the patient's benefit or time spent for the doctor's benefit? How will the patient experience it? Perhaps it depends on how it's done. Patients are less likely to react negatively to gathering such insurance information when the emphasis is on helping them decide if they can manage any possible copayment.

Similarly, if note taking will promote the likelihood that patients will get the insurance reimbursement that is needed, and this is explained, they are more likely to experience the note taking as a concern for their welfare. Times change, and as such practice demands change as well. The spirit of Greenson's attitude is crucial, but his particular style of practice may not be appropriate today. In keeping with the spirit, the current-day practitioner needs to keep in mind the importance of making certain that patients understand that their interests are being protected. An explanation of the benefit to the patient of note taking might accomplish the same goals that Greenson is emphasizing. A general rule might be to keep in mind the need for explaining procedures when the benefit to the patient cannot be understood in terms of common sense.

The point is, and I think I made myself clear, I'm against notes. At least in the initial interview. Incidentally, I take notes otherwise, from time to time, but this we will talk about when we get beyond the initial interview. In the initial interview, I have a total stranger, the whole world is open. I don't know what in the world he wants from me or what I'm going to do for him. I usually have a limited time in which to appraise him, and I want to give myself over to that task. At times I have even neglected to get an address. Okay, it's bad financially, but it's good in terms of the initial interview. I really devote it to the patient. Please, I say to the patient: react and let me observe, and I'm willing to participate.

*Candidate:* You say react because they really come in with everything.

*Greenson:* I don't say to the patient, "please react," it is in my attitude that I convey the sense, "I am at your disposal, I'm not giving up part of my interest to a notebook. I'm interested only in you. I won't answer the phone. I'm at your disposal. Here I am." This is what I like to impart to the patient in my attitude. So the notes have no place in my book, no place.[19]

[20] Here Greenson touches on an essential diagnostic concern that goes beyond the conceptual framework of the DSM. He is pointing out that treatment planning based on a diagnosis must include an assessment of the healthy parts of the patient as much as an assessment of the sick parts. Thus, as the reader goes through this section it is as important to consider each point of assessment for both sickness and health. It is as important to assess each healthy ego function as it is to find ego functions that have been compromised by sickness. What the patient can do is as important as what the patient cannot do. Clearly such considerations have long been the case in medicine, where treatments are often considered in light of the patient's relative state of well-being. Whatever the treatment procedure under consideration, it is crucial to ascertain the extent to which the patient possesses the capabilities of participating in the procedure.

# 3

# The Appraisal of
# the Patient

*Greenson:* Let's get on to the aims of the initial interviews. What are you trying to accomplish in initial interviews? I would break this down into two main aims: one, the appraisal of the patient, and by that I mean not just the diagnosis of the case. By this time you all know the diagnosis obsessive–compulsive character doesn't tell you anything about whether this man is analyzable, or at least it doesn't tell you enough. The diagnosis manic-depressive doesn't tell you enough; the diagnosis schizoid character doesn't tell you enough. The diagnosis hysteria, phobia, conversion doesn't tell you: Is this patient analyzable or not? Does he need psychotherapy, does he need hospitalization? Just a diagnosis doesn't give you enough real data. You want to do more than come to a diagnosis. You want to appraise the patient, which means not only his sickness but his healthy parts too.[20] The total picture of what this guy is. That's why I say appraisal.

## The Preliminary Appraisal

*Greenson:* And here I think the appraisal of the patient has to be divided into two big categories. One, the preliminary appraisal. By that I mean the essential question: Is this an emergency, or do I have time? The first question I want to answer when I see a patient is that question, is this urgent, is this a decompensation, is this an acute psychotic break, is this an overwhelming anxiety? If I have time, fine. I would do the whole thing completely differently if I've got the time. If it's an emergency, I handle the whole thing also very differently, you know you do the same thing. If it's an acute psychosis, or an acute hysteria, or an acute anxiety, anything acute and sudden and decompensating. If it's a schizophrenic, but an old one, okay, I have time. If it's a mild anxiety state, I have time. In other words, is this a case that's going to require hospitalization, medication, immediate support, or is this a case that's ambulatory, that I can do a certain amount of uncovering or catharsis with? Above all, before you can think in terms of what is the long-range view, in this preliminary appraisal you have to decide the short view; if this person needs immediate help right now or if it can wait. So that's the first appraisal.

## The Definitive Appraisal

*Greenson:* Once I have decided it's not an emergency case, then I can take my time and make a more careful appraisal, the definitive appraisal. What do you look for? It's your patient, gentlemen, what do you look for, how do you appraise a patient? Say you've got two hour's time, you know the patient can come twice, or you've got two free hours with the patient. What do you try to see, or look for? There are four factors which I have put down as essential. I mean now big factors. But it is your appraisal of the patient, so what do you look for? Go on.

*Candidate:* One would be their appearance, bearing, way of speaking, way of moving, facial grimaces, characteristics, their general body configuration, how they carry themselves—would be one thing I would look at in a case.

[21] Greenson later says that he spends from one to three hours for the initial interview. Nowadays practitioners may find that insurance will only reimburse one hour for an initial interview, although the pressures to justify the need for treatment may turn this into one hour to get the needed information for reimbursement rather than only one hour to gather information to decide on a treatment plan. Keep in mind, Greenson is talking about an assessment for psychoanalysis, whereas an assessment for a time-limited psychotherapy may not need to be as penetrating and comprehensive. By knowing how to do the most detailed initial interview techniques, however, the practitioner is in a position to know where modifications can be safely introduced. There is a much greater danger in doing more limited initial interviews because it is all one knows how to do.

[22] Greenson goes into more detail about motivation elsewhere (Greenson, 1979, pp. 30–36), but I will attempt to summarize what he has to say there. He observes that since the beginnings of psychoanalysis, patients seek treatment less and less for painful symptoms, and more and more for general complaints that life lacks meaning. He concludes that over time there are more patients seeking analysis with character disorders than with symptomatic disorders. In this section, he notes the importance of helping patients to recognize sources of suffering that may not be apparent to them. There are, for example, patients who avoid emotional distress at the cost of not living life nearly to the fullest, yet who fail to recognize what they are giving up.

Greenson also highlights a crucial distinction between symptomatic treatment, which is the emphasis of the managed care model (from a psychoanalytic point of view this includes the biological model, the cognitive–behavioral model, the behavioral model, etc.) as opposed to the psychoanalytic treatment model. He points out that it is the analyst's job to make sure a patient does not flee the challenges of treatment because they experience some immediate symptomatic relief. The analyst must help the patient stay in touch with sources of motivation to continue the treatment, lest some temporary relief lead the patient to settle for superficial results that will not last, or that fall far short of the patient's potential to live life fully. This means the patient must be helped to remain aware of the tendency to accept the status quo where psychological growth means facing sources of internal conflict.

The distinction between symptomatic cures and psychoanalytic cures is crucial. Psychoanalytic treatments aim to give patients greater freedom from the unconscious, inner conflicts that diminish their ability to live life as fully as possible. In this regard, Greenson points out that desperation by itself is a poor indication for analysis, and that it may not be possible to assess a patient's motivation for intensive, exploratory treatment until they have been helped out of their desperation.

*Greenson:* What else?

*Candidate:* I would want to know what is the core conflict, what is the patient coming for, or what has really happened to send him for help, and if possible to see in those few hours what he is really trying to deal with.[21]

*Greenson:* In other words, you are talking about the motivation[22] of the patient. You're talking about, I would say, the

Related to the patient's motivation, Greenson points out the need for patients to take *responsibility* for their own misery. Here we have a psychoanalytic view that is mistakenly seen as a great departure from the spirit of biological psychiatry, where the patient is encouraged to view psychiatric suffering as a "medical illness" rather than something that is their "fault." By *responsibility* Greenson does not mean the patient is at fault and should bear guilt for having an illness. He means the patient takes charge and accepts the tasks of doing what needs to be done to get better, which may include a willingness to endure distressing emotions revealed by the treatment process. This kind of personal responsibility is as important for biological psychiatry as it is for psychoanalysis, even though medication treatment makes far fewer emotional demands on the patient. The success of treatment with medications does depend on the patient responsibly reporting symptoms, taking the medications as prescribed, monitoring improvement, noting side effects, and then reporting back to the physician as required.

There are several other issues Greenson raises that will impact the motivation for treatment. He mentions the willingness to spend a considerable amount of time and money. He mentions the willingness to forego quick and temporary results for more thorough, lasting results, and he mentions the capacity to give up any secondary gains that are related to the illness. Greenson views some patients as getting so much from their illness that an intervention which threatens to remove those gains will not prove to be an acceptable option.

[23] Greenson will take this subject of psychological mindedness up later in this volume (pp. 147–157). Also, Ralph Greenson's son, Daniel Greenson, who is also a psychoanalyst, has written about psychological mindedness in a memorial volume dedicated to his father (D. Greenson, 1992). He mentions the following: a genuine interest in how the mind works, a capacity for insight, an interest in how others are put together, an interest in fantasy, an ability to conceptualize experiences as interconnected and meaningful, an ability to see oneself as others see one, and a sense that dreams are important psychologically.

ego functions in some way of the patient. I would certainly agree that the main thing you want to appraise above all is, what is the patient's capacity for ego functioning? The id gives you some clues, the superego gives you some clues, but none of them gives you the kind of clues that are important for what therapy he needs and how sick he is, what you've got to work with, and how treatable he is. Then the next point is, or one of the next points is, what are the patient's motivations? How much pain does he have from his symptom? How does it disturb him? How ego alien is it? Is he coming because he got caught by the police or his wife will divorce him, or is he miserable? There are two other important factors.

*Candidate:* The type of defenses that he employs or . . .

*Greenson:* That would be under the ego functions. I am getting at a whole new category.

*Candidate:* I wonder if maybe it's possible to make an interpretation, to see how he reacts, and to see if he has a capacity for insight.

*Greenson:* The next big category is, what is the psychological mindedness[23] of the patient. This has to do with such questions as, how does he react to confrontations, or an interpretation, how much empathy does this guy have? Because let us say his ego functions are pretty good, and let us say he is well motivated, but if he isn't psychologically minded it changes the whole complexion of what you want to do with him. So I think the third big category is the psychological mindedness of the patient. We will go into detail about each of these things. And the fourth one has to do with, what are the external factors. Can he pay, does he have the time, does he live in the city, does he come from San Bernadino, does he fly in from Mexico? I mean all these factors also play a role. So once the emergency appraisal is settled, emergency or no emergency, then comes the more careful appraisal which will include, I think, these four big categories:

[24] Here Greenson appears to react to the issue of whether or not it is important that there is a good interpersonal fit between doctor and patient. It is interesting to ask if the importance of such a good fit is as relevant in short-term psychotherapy treatment models as it is for psychoanalysis. Might it be more important? In reality, it is more and more the case in the managed care model, especially the health maintenance organization, that neither the patient nor the doctor has much choice about whom they will see. In an effort to equalize referrals amongst providers economically, managed care companies create policies that make referrals to specific providers difficult if not impossible. These policies disregard the possibility that all therapists and patients cannot work together with equal effectiveness.

From a psychoanalytic point of view, as Greenson notes, the fit between doctor and patient is a factor to consider in making treatment decisions. Unfortunately, the documentation of such factors is difficult in terms of traditional experimental models with statistical analysis, although recently, a series of articles did appear in the journal *Professional Practice: Research and Practice* (DeLeon, 1998) that document psychologists' perceptions that the intrusion of managed care into the clinical decision process is having a decidedly negative impact on quality of patient care. This impact is due to loss of control over clinical decisions and the erosion of confidentiality. Clearly along with the loss of control over clinical decisions, managed care has interfered with the freedom of doctors and patients to choose each other.

ego functions, psychological mindedness, motivation, external factors. So the big aim of the initial interview is appraisal of the patient. What is the only other important aim of the initial interview?

*Candidate:* What about, do I want to see his patient?

*Greenson:* Hmmm, it never occurred to me. That's true. Do I want the patient, is the patient for me?[24] I suppose that ought to be included.

*Candidate:* Not only is the patient for me—am I for the patient?

# 4 | The Initial Interviews Have to Be Therapeutic

*Greenson:* But that's not the thing I'm going to decide right off the bat. Okay, but that does raise a third point, one other point is that the initial interviews have to be therapeutic. I think this is too often neglected. I see patients on Friday mornings from 8:00 A.M. to 10 A.M. at the Veterans Hospital. I'm supposed to interview them for the medical students. I want to tell you, every one of those interviews is therapeutically beneficial to the patient. They get something out of it. Not only do I not do damage at the least, but I make a point of trying to be helpful to the patient, even in the first hour that I see them.

*Candidate:* How do you do this in front of the students?

*Greenson:* Well, for example, after being very constricted with me a man eventually pours out some of his troubles and I usually make some statement like, you ought to do more of this group therapy, and he will say, what the hell,

[25] Here Greenson is addressing the fact that patients do not uniformly reveal what their problems are. This is a crucial fact to keep in mind when working in short-term, managed care models that assume symptomatic checklists will tell the patient's story. Greenson is also pointing out that it is important for patients to leave the initial interview feeling they have been helped in some way. In the passages that follow he discusses what he means by the terms *therapeutic* and *helpful* so as to address concerns about compromising the analytic setting.

[26] It will become increasingly apparent that by "therapeutically beneficial" Greenson means doing something that patients will experience as improving their inner state. While there are many possible ways a patient might feel relief, the therapeutic benefit of the initial interview might be some immediate recommendations, some assurance that the problems are treatable, or the reassurance that can come from being with someone who really listens and cares.

Greenson clearly takes a stance against notions that psychoanalytic evaluations should be conducted with a detached, observational, quasi-scientific attitude. He clearly is more concerned with establishing a relationship of trust and hope than with protecting analytic neutrality or being analytically abstinent. For Greenson, the analytic process does not need to be "protected" from directly letting patients know that we are there to be helpful. As a result, the alliance with the patient is built more upon real, direct sources of assurance from the first contacts, rather than being built primarily upon idealizations that are forced to hide in shadows. Greenson would not recommend such interventions if he felt that they would muddy the analytic relationship and encumber the treatment process. This is consistent with his strong adherence to the importance of establishing and maintaining an alliance with the patient that is not reducible to transference.

I don't have much I can talk about there. Then I will say, participate more, I think you're keeping things back.[25] But it's really crucial to realize, no matter what your aim is, like you want to know the patient or you want to know the diagnosis, this is a sick person in trouble who is coming for help, and dammit it's up to you to give him some help, even if it's a little, but to give him some help in the initial interview. And I must say I find many, many analysts and candidates very negligent in this. They feel, well, in coming to me he only wants to know what I think of him. Nonsense, he's coming because he's in trouble and he's in pain and it ought to be therapeutically beneficial for him. It may be painful. I don't mean don't hurt him, but it should be therapeutically beneficial.[26]

*Candidate:* Do you intend to follow up later on what you mean by "therapeutically beneficial"?

*Greenson:* Yes, I will give you concrete illustrations of this.

*Candidate:* Because I think it means, not to be more harmful in the long run than helpful, so it depends on what your aims are.

*Greenson:* Now one second, don't give me double talk. What do you mean that this can be more harmful than helpful?

*Candidate:* I think we first have to clarify what we mean by being therapeutic.

*Greenson:* Now one second. What's the puzzle here? What's the puzzle about being therapeutically helpful?

*Candidate:* For example, to one person being therapeutic might mean to give advice. To another person it might mean to make a suggestion to change something, any of which might be wrong in terms of some later understanding.

*Greenson:* Go slowly, any of which may be wrong in terms of what?

[27] Here the candidate raises a very important issue. First impressions, based on the initial interview, do not always stand the test of time. Greenson replies by saying he clearly wishes to be helpful. He does not advocate "wild therapy." It is interesting to consider these issues in light of the current interest in "empirically validated, manualized psychotherapies." Such treatments are rigorously prescriptive, they are based on descriptive DSM assessments, and they aim to treat symptoms not unconscious, dynamic factors. For this reason, they probably do not meet Greenson's criteria of wild therapy, even though they are interventions that may be decided upon in half an hour. On the other hand, patients can misrepresent their symptoms for a variety of conscious and unconscious reasons, which makes the descriptive, symptomatic approach vulnerable to misleading first impressions.

Greenson is concerned, however, with psychodynamic assessment and treatment, where it is clearly understood that initial impressions can be quite misleading. The therapist is trying to assess much more subtle, underlying issues. Amongst the various factors that complicate the therapist's first impressions, Greenson offers a useful discussion of the patient meeting the therapist for the first time with "a mixture of transference based and realistic expectations" (Greenson, 1967). He goes on to say:

> Only those methods of approach which seem understandable to the patient may lead to realistic reactions in the patient. My "analyst personality" as it is manifested in the first interviews may also stir up both transference and realistic reactions. It is my impression that those qualities which seem strange or threatening or non-professional will evoke strong transference reactions along with anxiety. Those traits which the patient believes indicate a therapeutic intent, compassion, and expertness may produce realistic responses as well as positive transference reactions [p. 204].

In a few words here, "therapeutic intent, compassion, and expertness" Greenson has captured the importance of the therapist conveying to the patient, "I am interested in finding the best way to help you—I care about you—and I am competent." He views these three messages as essential in fostering realistic responses, a positive transference and a spirit essential to a healthy working alliance.

Greenson (1967, p. 51) also points out that in assessing readiness for psychoanalysis there are many considerations to take into account, some having to do with assessing the patient's total life circumstances and others having to do with assessing the patient's total personality. He points out that it is just not possible to assess all these factors in one session. In the upcoming example, notice how he even considers that a trial of psychoanalysis may be the most reliable indicator that it is the treatment of choice for a given patient.

*Candidate:* The further understanding of the patient's problems. That is, I think what we're assuming is that the analyst in a half an hour gets some understanding, and he may want to do something, but it might be the wrong move in terms of what they ultimately decide needs work.[27]

*Greenson:* In other words, short-range help to the patient may be in the long range harmful for some ultimate aim.

*Candidate:* It depends on what you learn about the patient later.

*Greenson:* Yes, I can see that. And I think there is some danger, but I nevertheless feel your aim ought to be, at least you must consider wanting to be helpful to the patient. I agree that the fact that the patient may potentially become a patient of yours, or become a patient of anybody's, will influence how much you feel you may or may not do. I don't think in the initial interview it should be necessary or advisable to make an intervention that would be harmful in a long-range view. I don't believe in doing wild therapy.[28]

---

[28] Here Greenson coins the term *wild therapy* from the term *wild analysis,* which originated with Freud's article devoted to " 'Wild' Psycho-Analysis'' (Freud, 1910, p. 221). In this succinct, eight-page article Freud delineates several ways in which interpretations can be incorrect, untimely, and ineffective. Where timing is concerned, Freud worried about psychoanalysts wanting to hasten the treatment process by attempting to circumvent resistances. He worried about analysts applying a superficial understanding of psychoanalytic theory in a didactic fashion, again to get more rapid results. It appears that Greenson is referring to similar concerns in his efforts to restrict what he means by being "helpful" to the patient in the first meeting.

[29] The fact that Greenson insists on using fictitious names that sound like real, live people is a good example of his concern that patients not be dehumanized, and his ever-present focus on treating clinical material and patients with the utmost respect and care. It also appears to be part of his efforts to help his students grasp the patient's frame of reference, so they will establish and maintain an empathic perspective.

*Candidate:* This is why I think you have to define what you mean by being therapeutic.

*Greenson:* Being helpful. For example, let me give an illustration. I described Joe Berkowitz. Incidentally, I hate giving names of anonymous patients like Joe Jones, because they seem dead.[29] I would rather give names that sound alive like Joe Berkowitz or Betty Glassman. I don't know anybody named Betty Glassman or Joe Berkowitz, so that's all right, but if you happen to know anyone with these names, they are not who I mean, you're grasping at straws. It's not who I mean. I just would rather call anonymous people by names that seem a little bit alive than by saying Joe Jones or something like John Smith. But Joe Berkowitz, let me describe this man and how the interview . . .

*Candidate:* . . . he's sick . . .

*Greenson:* . . . he's quite sick, Joe Berkowitz, this guy I described, this Rilke-looking figure, who wants to be a playwright and is plagued by doing well in school. Now he told me then that he'd had some individual psychotherapy in Stockbridge, for I think two years, and then he had one year of psychotherapy up in Berkeley. Now all this was fact finding, incidentally, and I listened to all this. I then got some information about his parents. His father had died in an accident and his mother had died, I don't remember from what, carcinoma I believe. He had been an orphan now for some years although he was a young man of 23 or 24.

I was taken a little bit aback by Stockbridge because that's a sanitarium, and he was there for two years and had one year of psychotherapy. So I asked him, then tell me, when you went up to Berkeley you had psychotherapy there? He said, yes; I said, well, how often did you see your therapist? He said five times a week. I said sitting up? He said yes. Then I said, how do you feel now? What kind of therapy are you interested in now? He said, well, I'm not sure, I don't know, but maybe, I don't know, maybe I ought to try

[30] For the reader who may not be familiar with the psychoanalytic use of the term *confrontation*, it may appear as if Greenson is talking about being hostile. In psychoanalytic parlance, however, there are three kinds of interventions, which are referred to as clarifications, confrontations, and interpretations. A clarification is a request for more detail, a confrontation questions assumptions, and an interpretation points out something that lies outside of a patient's awareness. Thus, a confrontation is likely to be more stressful for a patient than a clarification.

psychoanalysis. Now here I could have ducked the whole issue since I knew I was not going to take him as a patient. I had no time. I was going to refer him elsewhere. But I felt that my ducking this would let some anxiety grow in him. He would look at me wondering what is Greenson thinking, and I felt that by ducking this issue I would create more anxiety for him. But, by at least temporarily and superficially facing the issue, I thought I could be really of some therapeutic help to this man. So I said to him: Well, what makes you think now you are ready to do analysis, whereas before these other people didn't think you were ready? Now this was a calculated risk. Nevertheless I had talked to him for about twenty minutes, about half an hour, and had the feeling he isn't overly psychotic and he doesn't look even particularly too borderline, but that look, that Rilke look I said he had. So I asked, what makes you think now?

I was taking this calculated risk for two reasons, but one of them was therapeutic. I felt if I confronted[30] him that directly it would be therapeutically beneficial, and I was gratefully surprised when he said: Well, certain things are different with me now. He said, first of all, I have a girl friend, I'm getting along very well with her, and it's the first time in my life that I've been able to maintain any kind of a relationship with a girl friend. Second, although I'm still getting A's in school, which was always a problem (incidentally, interesting problem, huh?), I'm not obsessed by school like I was, I'm able to forget about school from time to time. Third, although there is still some tendency in me to get into accidents, I haven't had any major accidents for a while, and he recounted several things. I said, well, I must say from what you tell me now, when I hardly know you, that you may be right, maybe at this point you would be ready for analysis. But you know that it might not be determined until one gets to know you better, and then I suppose it will take some kind of a trial period before that really can be decided, whether you are ready for it. Now I think this whole intervention of confronting him with an anxiety which I think was bothering him, by being very forthright and direct about

it, by giving him some reassurance that analysis sounded plausible; that this was of therapeutic benefit to him.

*Candidate:* I think a doubt could be raised about this intervention. Could I raise it? We assume that the way you said it here was the way you said it to the patient, but it could have had another effect. What if you said: look here, you were up in Stockbridge two years, one year in Berkeley, what makes you think now you can have psychoanalysis?

*Greenson:* If I said it the way you did, it would really be traumatic to the patient.

*Candidate:* Well, I tried listening while you were saying it, and I was thinking, what if the patient had no good things, like what if there was really no positive change.

*Greenson:* I think you heard my words, but I don't think you heard some of the things which were expressed by the tone of my words. I felt after I talked to this man a half an hour, that he was in pretty good shape. Therefore I felt being bold in directly confronting him would be beneficial to him. Now, although I felt that, I realized there was some risk. Therefore, I was pleasantly surprised and delighted when he took it up very nicely and said, Well, there are certain things that have changed. I want to say, I am against being bold when the odds are against me, but I am very much in favor of being bold when the odds are in favor of me. I am very much opposed to being cautious when caution frightens a patient. Now again, maybe I'm excusing a character trait of mine, as my character would be to take the risk of being bold rather than take the risk of being cautious. Let us assume there is a risk in being bold, but let us also face the fact that there is also a risk in being cautious. A patient picks it up, don't think they don't because they do. I would rather be if anything a little bolder than a little more cautious. It is my nature. Since it is my nature, I suppose I'm willing to say, it is less dangerous and there are less drawbacks to it.

So again, you know this is a personally loaded opinion that I'm giving you, but my feeling about initial interviews with such patients, the fact that this man had come to see me, the fact that he had been referred to me for analysis, the way I appraised him in the first half hour of that interview, all made me feel that it would be beneficial for me to be quite direct with him, to ask him these questions, and to see how he reacted. I felt my boldness was therapeutically helpful to him. I think it took a load off him. I think he would have been very anxious if I hadn't broached it at all. Now perhaps I could have played it safe as you would suggest, which would not be so bold but would be to say, sort of noncommittally: Well now, have any changes taken place in you since you were last seen in Berkeley (not in Stockbridge, which was just some months ago). I could have been sort of noncommittal instead of being more direct, but I think I was more direct because I sensed his anxiety about the question. So I put it into words and asked in a way that assumed he had reasons to think he could now be analyzed.

I sent him to someone, incidentally, who saw him. I passed on a letter that was sent to me from Stockbridge, which was a very brief note, and then said, I thought this man might be analyzed, but I said I had questions because there must be a reason he had all this psychotherapy without analysis. Later I spoke to the analyst who said, "I think he probably can be analyzed, but I'm taking my time. I'm seeing him five times a week, but I'm so far having him sit up and I have seen him four or five hours now, sitting up." I agreed with him, and said I would take my sweet time myself in getting him on the couch. I would want to see how far off he goes when he goes off, or does he go off, and does he lose contact.

Now there's an example where I would say I really did something more than getting a history from this guy or sending him to someone. I try to make this a point with every patient I see: to do something or at least to keep in mind that I want the patient to leave the hour with some kind of benefit, even if it only means that I tell the patient I don't have enough time in the hour to do more than

[31] In this passage, Greenson makes several important points. First, conducting an initial interview with caution has the same risk–benefit potential for a patient as being bold. In other words, being cautious can be harmful. Second, it can be as therapeutic to increase emotional distress as it can be to relieve it. And third, when a therapist has to choose between different interview styles, there are advantages to choosing styles that are congenial to the therapist's personality. Since Greenson's focus is on the idea that even the initial interview should be therapeutic, it is a kind of thinking that can be applied to the managed care model as much as psychoanalytic treatments. The patient should benefit from the first meeting as well as subsequent meetings.

ask some questions. The diagnostic interview has this great disadvantage of emphasizing the appraisal, or emphasizing the referral instead of realizing that, my God, here's a chance to do something for the patient; it doesn't have to be great, you don't have to make interpretations or give them new insights. Even if you just structure something or formulate something or condense something or reaffirm something, it should be done with the question: Is this going to help him or is this going to disturb him? Now it may be for some patients it will be necessary or advisable to stir up some anxiety in this interview. You know, I don't want to give you the impression that being therapeutically helpful only means allaying anxiety; it may well be that from the therapeutic point of view something that creates anxiety is beneficial.[31]

*Candidate:* Or simply some small statements to let them know that they are understood can be made in very subtle ways.

*Greenson:* Certainly. Again I don't want to give you the impression that these are great interventions that are done. The example I showed was a pretty mild one. I just confronted the patient, and said, What makes you believe this? I'm trying to think of some other recent ones. The one I did in the hospital, for example, which is not even an analytic interview; it's in front of a class. This man has been in the hospital since World War II. I think he's had fifty admissions since 1944. My therapeutic intervention with him was after I got some history with him and said: My God, what makes you think that you have to give up trying to make a go of it outside? You're still young, you're energetic, you're intelligent, you've got brains, why are you giving up? You sound resigned, defeated, why? And I said this in a kind of an aggressive way, though this was the first time I ever saw the man. I said, I think you're not trying enough with the group therapy (because that's all they're offering him at the Veterans). I think you'd get a lot more out of it if you really tried.

[32] Here Greenson gives an example of being therapeutic by, in a sense, caring about the patient more than the patient seems to care about himself. He portrays the work of the psychotherapist as involving passions as well as ideas. But most of all, he is letting the students know how much he values the establishment of a real, caring relationship from the initial contacts.

This is a challenge for therapists who work for insurance companies. How to fill out the needed paperwork without allowing the forms to come between the patient and the therapist? How to make sure that patient and therapist are together fulfilling whatever insurance requirements must be done? Greenson is not a snob, he recognizes that patients may not have access to optimal approaches to treatment, but he advocates for the patient doing as much as is possible in the given system. Thus, for this patient, he says if it's not possible to get individual therapy, do all you can for yourself in group therapy.

I would try if I were you to get some more individual therapy, but if that's not possible, at least give more in the group. Certainly no great intervention, but this is not a guinea pig. This is not a dog set up before the class. It's a human being in pain and suffering! I'm supposed to use him for demonstration purposes, but I was demonstrating the initial interview, and I was going to show these first-year medical students, here's how I do it. I tried to appraise the patient, I tried to determine many things, but also I kept in mind the fact that I'm a doctor and he's a patient and I want to help him.[32]

*Candidate:* There is something very crucial in what you're saying, raised over and over again, having to do with whether you're with him [the patient] or not.

[33] The idea of establishing an object relationship with a patient is different from Greenson's ideas about the working alliance (Greenson, 1967, pp. 206–208). The working alliance is a special variety of object relationship that Greenson felt was "a relatively rational, desexualized, and de-aggressified transference phenomena." By contrast, here Greenson appears to be talking about establishing an interaction that includes mutual involvement rather than merely interview and observation. He wants to see how patients respond when he makes genuine attempts to relate to them, as opposed to treating them like specimens.

A second issue raised here is the use of the word *object*, which is a holdover from early psychoanalytic theory that most analysts find unfortunate but unavoidable. Here Greenson uses the term in a very loose manner when he refers to "object relationship," as its various meanings are most often reserved for intrapsychic not interpersonal meanings. When Greenson refers to "object relations" he is talking about the world of relationships that exists in the mind, which impacts but is different from the world of interpersonal relationships.

# 5

## How Do You Establish an Object Relationship?

**You Must Be More than an Observer**

*Greenson:* All right. This leads me to what I think is the heart of the matter. If you were to ask what is the crux of the initial interview situation, what's the heart of the matter, my answer would be: The crux of the initial interview situation is to establish an object relationship with your patient in which you then have a sample of observing the patient's capacity for object relations.[33] Now the way you do that is not by being an interviewer and observer. You must in part become a participant. The crux of the matter of how to conduct an initial interview is, get away from just being the observer. Establish an object relationship, which means partly become a participant with this patient, partly an observer. By establishing the object relationship, in addition to the data he will be betraying his physical behavior, his speech, his affects, his movements, his poise, his posture, in addition to that you will get one additional factor, his capacity and way of making an object relationship. You will get very valuable data from that.

57

If you want to know what's new about initial inter-viewing, this is what's new. It's the only thing that's new. Realize that in the initial interview you have to establish an object relationship, which means you cannot be the with-drawn, passive observer. You must do some degree of partici-pating—to what degree we'll discuss because you have to be careful not to go too much—but to some degree you must become a participant. Once you are with him, he will react and show you lots of things he would never show you if you are the observer. If you sit there behind your desk with a poker face, you will miss many important nuances that you will only get if you are partly a participant with the patient.

Well, this is the heart of the matter. By establishing the object relationship you have a most valuable way of testing the ego functions. Look, you can test ego functions by saying to the patient, what time is it, what day is it, where are you, how old are you, and if he's any kind of patient he'll spit in your eye. If he's worth his salt, he will not do it. How much better you can get this information by establishing a rela-tionship with this man, and not having to ask these ques-tions. By establishing an object relation with the patient, I don't mean that I initiate and take the lead and maintain the lead in actively doing something with this patient, I don't mean that. What I mean is permitting an object rela-tionship or facilitating an object relationship to be estab-lished. I think that's more correct. And, I would say, I facilitate the establishment of an object relationship be-tween me and the patient in the initial interview. I facilitate. I place no obstacles in the way, and I do certain things even perhaps under certain circumstances to encourage it or even to initiate it.

## You Must Help the Patient to Feel at Ease

I will spell it out for you when we go to the technique of it, but let's face it, the way I open the door, or you open the door, and the way you greet your patient, you're starting it. You can open the door with the dead pan, the smile of the

[34] It is important to keep in mind that this was said in 1959, at a time when cigarette smoking was far more commonplace and the hazards of it were not widely known, even amongst physicians.

[35] Although Greenson uses a male patient for this example, clearly these issues pertain equally to male and female patients.

inscrutable East upon the face, or you can open the door with a friendly look on your face. I don't think I open the door with any more of a bounce than most people open the door ordinarily. I make a point when I open the door for a new patient, to go out to the door and say, I'm Dr. Greenson, you must be Mr. Berkowitz—I'm still stuck with Joe Berkowitz—how do you do, please come in. I could come out and just say nothing, but I don't, I say who I am. We walk into the room. I say, please have a seat. There are two seats he could choose. I give him a choice. He takes one of the two seats. I don't care which, and then I sit down. I usually light a cigarette, therefore I always offer him a cigarette.[34] These are, for example, activities I do. I think they facilitate the establishment of an object relationship. Now you will say they must have transference complications, they certainly may have, but all of them in themselves are perfectly analyzable reactions in this man's future analysis, if he's going to be analyzed by me or anybody else. I'm the host, he is my guest, and it is how I would greet anyone at the door who was sent to me.[35]

*Candidate:* There is little point in clarifying. I think everything you have done we all do, or at least we should do.

*Greenson:* Wait a minute, don't say we all do. I don't know that everybody does.

*Candidate:* This might be termed in such a way as: What are the human relationships you establish with a patient, these are initial things, there must be many things that go on for the next 48 minutes.

## You Must Permit Your Wish to Help the Patient

*Greenson:* What goes on in the next 48 minutes is essentially permitting myself a certain amount of responsiveness. I would say essentially what I consider facilitating is permitting myself responsiveness and I would say not facilitating would be not permitting myself responsiveness. I don't play

[36] From the perspective of technique, Greenson touches on issues of technique that have a long history of controversy and confusion. Freud wrote his technique papers during the period of his topographic model of the mind, when the analyst's task was to help the patient overcome repressions and bring material into consciousness. It was not until the shift to the structural model that object relations became a significant part of the theory, yet Freud never went back to revise his earlier technical recommendations. As a result, the theory of technique has tended to lag behind other aspects of theory. Here Greenson is making a strong statement about the therapeutic relationship, and his feeling that therapists who play a role and attempt to suppress the wish to be helpful will have trouble establishing a relationship, which will make it difficult if not impossible to evaluate the patient's capacity to form a relationship.

a role. This is the way I am, and it so happens I feel this way toward my patients, fortunately. But above all never play a role. I don't think one should ever do that, play a role. I find it most obnoxious and very dangerous. But I feel that the wish to help people is an innate tendency in people who become doctors in the first place, and it usually lasts after you have been analyzed. It's permissible to want to help, although it does get knocked out of many people after years of analysis. You get the notion that this is wrong, that you're really supposed to be the recorder of his unconscious and the decoder of it. Nevertheless, some of us still have the feeling that it's permissible to want to help patients, and I think I let some of this come through without being a great rescuer on a white horse coming to save a patient from a dragon.[36]

[37] This section has important implications for those therapists in contemporary practices with managed care companies that require extensive forms be filled out, sometimes even before the initial interview. How much are therapists' impressions shaped by information that precedes contact with the patient? Greenson does note that when he only has one hour for the initial interview, he likes to have more information from other sources, on the grounds that one hour is "awfully skimpy" and does not allow for gathering much information. For example, how does the patient respond when returning to a familiar situation the second time, as compared to the first visit?

# 6

## How Much Do You Want to Know Before You See the Patient?[37]

*Greenson:* I want to go back to the question that I think you raised about the referring psychoanalyst, how much do you want to know about the patient before you see him? That's an interesting question, because you feel that there is a disadvantage in knowing too much about someone else's view. Is that right? Do you really feel that in some cases knowing too much would interfere with your appraisal of the patient? Is that right?

*Candidate:* Knowing too much could promote biases.

*Greenson:* I think that is right. There's no doubt that a complicated, long, and detailed history of the patient certainly interferes with the freshness of your own impressions. Don't you all agree that it would be best to avoid a detailed history of a patient that you're going to see? On the other hand, would you feel that getting sort of a thumbnail sketch of the patient would be disadvantageous?

*Candidate:* No, but I think the urge of the referring person is always to give his impressions of the highlights of the case, sometimes with a lot of detail.

*Greenson:* I can see that a long and detailed history about a patient would influence you and bias your spontaneous reactions so that you might in an initial interview, then tend to weigh certain things on the basis of the history that you got rather than on your own impressions, if they were purely fresh. I can see that. I can also see, however, that you might not have been alert enough to certain aspects of the case, as you would if you had gotten a kind of a thumbnail sketch that would give some highlights and some conclusions. In other words, let me say a man is referred to me, and I'm trying to think of an actual case. I can't offhand. I got a letter just today, from an analyst in New York who said, I'm sending you this patient. He gave me a brief history of the man, a young man, a college student, graduate of Harvard, went to medical school, quit medical school, is now working in his father's business. And he said this is a brilliant schizophrenic boy but he's done a lot of good work, and so on.

Now I already have the preconceived notion that this man, according to this analyst, is a schizophrenic boy. But there were not enough details in there and not enough pressure in this letter to really oppress me. I think I will still see him with relative freshness since the image I have of him is relatively unformed, yet I am alert to the possibility, is he schizophrenic? This analyst who referred him to me incidentally wrote in her letter to me: "I think he needs analysis, I think he can be analyzed." So I'm alert now to this question, I feel this amount of information is rather helpful, it's not hurtful. That's my impression. If there had been a very long letter I think I would have skipped through it very skimpily, not read it in great detail, gotten the highlights, and seen the patient. Then after I saw the patient I'd go back and read the letter. I think if she had not written me the letter and I had seen this man, it's conceivable that I could have missed some of the dangerous implications of this case.

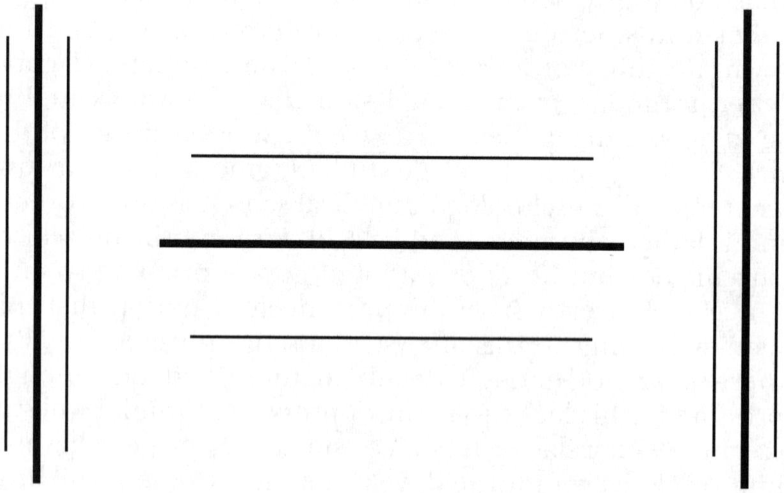

I certainly know that in interviewing applicants for psychoanalytic training, candidates, all of us have missed real pathology, all of us; of course in those days we used to do it without reading the reports of anybody else, we just did it cold. Now we have a new system. We have a five-man admissions committee and we circulate the letters to one another, so that often you get the letter before you see the man. It is interesting, many of us don't read the letters of other people. We get the letters and won't read them. We just read the conclusion in order not to be too influenced, and yet it's helpful to get sort of a general notion of what the other person thinks. Now some of us have read the letters and then said, you know I was influenced by the other person's letter, that's why I weighed him in this particular direction. There's a danger in getting too much information and letting it influence you, but it can be helpful to get a small amount of information or indications that can make you more alert, particularly if you are limited in the amount of time you can give to the initial interview. If I have three, four, or five hours for initial interview, I would rather have nothing at all on the patient, but if I have one hour, then it's really helpful to have some other information. I find one hour awfully skimpy and many times I must make a referral or make some kind of temporary decision within one hour. I don't know what your feelings are about it. What's your experience of getting outside material during the course of treatment of a patient?

*Candidate:* My question is how do you shut off the referring person who wants to tell you all this information.

## What to Do with Information That Arrives Before the Patient?

*Greenson:* Well if it's a referring man you could have a real problem; if it's a colleague, all right, you hope he understands this. It's a real problem and I absolutely agree with you, it is a burden to get data about the patient which the

patient has not yet uncovered to you. I deal with it in the initial interview. After I say to the patient, sit down, have a cigarette, have a seat, I always say, Dr. so-and-so called me about you and told me this. I always start by telling the patient what I know. I don't tell all the details, because that would either be too long, or I don't want to be pinned down to the exact details, but I give sort of a brief and superficial resume of what Dr. so-and-so said. I always start out by telling the patient a brief summary of what I know. First of all because I think otherwise I will betray it in some way, and I don't want that burden of having to keep a secret from the patient. But above all, I want the patient very early to know I don't keep secrets, and I don't want them to keep secrets. The two of us are here and it's for keeps, and professional ethics is secondary to: You are my patient and I am your doctor. I like this established very early in the treatment. You and I working together. This is what Dr. so-and-so told me. Now I won't go and say, he said you are a son of a bitch who never pays your bills, but within reason I'll say what the patient can bear and I'll say what I think is important that he knows I know. But does your question also have to do with the fact that during the course of the initial interviews the parents will come, or the husband will come, or something like that?

*Candidate:* I'm talking about information gathered in the beginning from the referring man which is much more detailed than you need to know in the initial interviews.

*Greenson:* That's a real problem, and I would either try to discourage the referring man from giving it to you, or if he gives it to you, I would try to tell it to the patient at the proper time, but I don't really know how you handle it better than that. Now maybe I don't get these kind of referrals. I haven't run into it recently that someone has burdened me with a lot of data about the patients, but sometimes I will tell you I have gotten phone calls and referrals which have been real difficult. I'll get a phone call from a doctor saying, I want to send you a patient, and she doesn't want to come but now she's been forced to come. Oy Vey! Why?

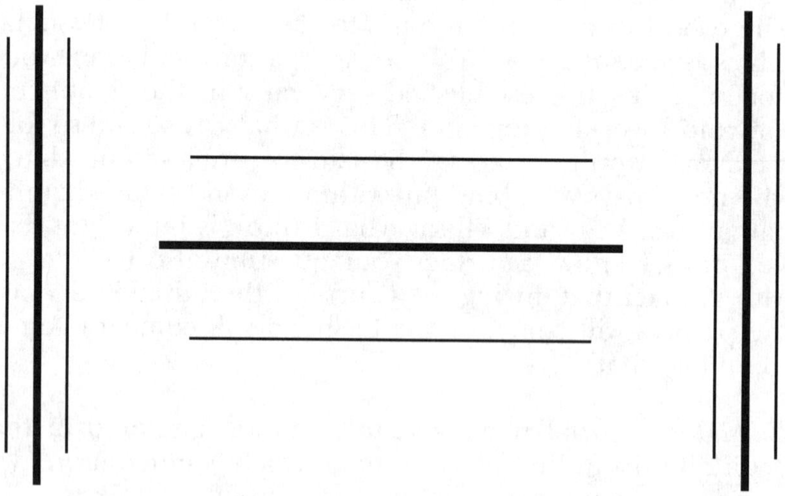

Because her husband says that if she doesn't go, he's walking out. What's her problem? Well she has a tendency to get drunk and when she gets drunk she urinates in the glasses. This interested me I must say. I said, she what? He said, "That's right, she gets drunk and when she gets drunk she goes and pees in all the glasses, which upsets the husband." And then he said, "and the next morning she denies the whole thing; she says she doesn't remember and it's not true."

I must say I felt this case was a challenge. I said, well, if you get her up here, I'm willing at least to see her. Now that was a ticklish point, she came in to see me, and I said Dr. so-and-so referred you. I wasn't going to start out by saying, he says you pee in glasses. I did it with more tact, and said, he says you have some problems with drinking, but before I could finish, she said: "Oh, I don't know what they're talking about. I just got drunk once, I drank too much, I wasn't really drunk." And I let her go on and talk and talk, and after a while I stopped her and said, but you know, he said that he understood you did certain things when you were drinking that were certainly not the kind of things you would do when you were sober. She put on this act of innocence and said, "I don't have any memory of it." I was really reluctant to say more as I had forgotten to ask who saw her do it, how do they know she did it? I'd forgotten to ask the doctor this, and she denied the whole thing in the first interview. I decided not to press the point until I called him back to get filled in on how he found out that she did it, how did the husband know it? The truth was the husband never saw it, but the maid saw it.

It was a really delicate problem to confront her with, but the second time I saw her I confronted her with it. I said, you know they said that when you got drunk you did a lot of things, a lot of things that kids sometimes do, I phrased it that way. She didn't take it, didn't follow it up. I said yes, they said that you urinated. I still didn't say in the glasses. I was being sort of delicate. It was incidentally the best china that she had. And she said, "Oh that's ridiculous, I never heard of such a thing." But I then pressed the point

[38] This passage gets to the important issue of tactful confrontation: How to penetrate beyond the surface and move the interview into areas that are likely to stir up distress, without provoking an unnecessary, irreparable disruption in the relationship with the patient? With more and more pressure on therapists to do their work in a shorter time frame, there is increasing danger of prematurely barging in on the patient's privacy or of failing to pursue key areas and never getting at the important issues.

a little bit more and said, well, it was told to me that after the party you went around taking the chinaware and urinated into the china. She protested very strongly about it, but I could tell that she was guilty about it. If she had really been innocent, she would have really protested, probably walked out of the office, said you're impossible, you're out of your mind, or whatever, but she didn't. Well I never really got her to admit it, incidentally. I saw her a few more times, but I never got her to admit it.[38] However, I did get her to stop drinking. Apparently she was so frightened that I had known about it that she stopped drinking. I haven't seen her since.

*Candidate:* The husband couldn't confront her with it?

*Greenson:* He didn't want to confront her with it.

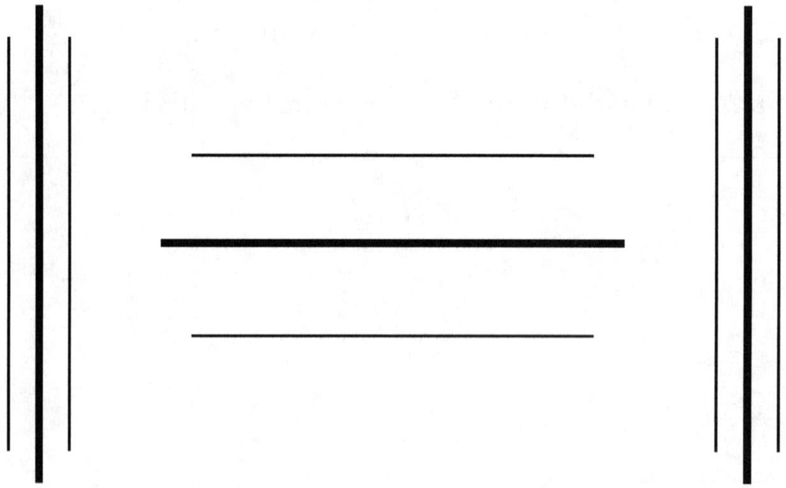

# 7 ‖ How to Handle the Initial Phone Call

*Greenson:* Five minutes more, if you don't mind, about how to handle the initial phone call. The first thing that starts off the initial interview is usually a phone call. Is there any special problem or any method or way you handle the phone call, anything special about it? Let's say the referring doctor says, "I want to make an appointment for her, she's right here in the office." I always say, please have her call me, right? You always have the patient call. Why? If she wants to run away, let her run away then. Don't make him tie her down, then he's made the appointment, not her. If her husband calls and says, I want to make an appointment for my wife, I say, please have your wife call. If the wife calls, I say, please have your husband call. I don't make appointments through a third party, unless it's a child. I want to confront them on the phone, if they have that much resistance, what's the use of trying to buck it. But now let us say the patient calls.

[39] Although it is over four decades since Greenson gave these lectures, and in some ways fee issues have changed, in other ways they are very much the same. For example, managed care has meant that more patients come to treatment with prearranged fees, but it has also meant more patients need to pay for their own treatment, in particular psychoanalytic treatments, since they are often no longer covered by insurance at all.

*Candidate:* What do you do if the husband calls and says, it's too hard for her to call, she asked me to call to make the appointment. She has a phobia.

*Greenson:* If she has a phone phobia, that's something else. All right, I would concede to that. Of course, when they're too sick that's something else. But when it is something where a husband is using pressure to manipulate the situation because she has too much resistance, I think these cases have a very poor prognosis, and I would rather not concede. You may feel differently about it. But let's say the patient calls. Any general rules about how you handle phone calls?

*Candidate:* I have some patients who call and just announce themselves, I am Mrs. so-and-so, and then they seem to wait for me to acknowledge them and recognize them.

*Greenson:* I don't think I have had that happen to me but I certainly think I would do the same, I would say "I'm Dr. Greenson," your move, and I probably would say it on the phone: "Your move." It might take five years of analysis later to analyze this, but I probably would say it: "Your move." I don't like that business of I am so-and-so, now do something.

## Being Asked the Fee Over the Phone[39]

*Greenson:* I expect to be treated with a certain amount of consideration. I resent bitterly patients on the phone saying, Dr. Greenson, could you tell me what is your fee. I resent it enormously. I don't know how you feel about it. I resent being asked the fee over the phone. I'm always tempted to give one answer. I have never done it, but some day in a temper I probably will say it, if I know the patient isn't poor. Because I have had patients who said, "I was referred to you by so-and-so of Hilltop Country Club; incidentally, doctor, what is your fee?" If I know the patient is loaded and he asks what my fee is, I'd like to say, well, today Greenson is selling for $5.00 a pound, how many pounds do you want?

[40] Although Greenson is clearly discussing a personal, emotional reaction, as a teacher he is not making his personal reaction the primary basis for education. In fact, he goes on to agree with a candidate who suggests a rational response to questions about fee on the phone. He even goes on to admit that his emotional reaction is his own problem. This is the stuff of great teaching, since Greenson simultaneously shows his students they have good ideas and he is fallible. Such teaching methods help students overcome the idealization of role models that can hamper the freedom to be creative, in part by simultaneously giving the students permission to be fallible.

I've never done it yet but I'm awfully tempted to do it. But that's a really tough one, what do you do when a patient says on the phone, what is your fee? I find it a very difficult situation. What do you do? Really, what do you do? Come on, you've all had that experience, what do you do?[40]

*Candidate:* I think the fee is something that until we know more about the situation, what is involved, it's not the proper time to discuss it.

*Greenson:* That's a very good answer. I can't answer your question about my fee until I know more about you, it's a very good answer. I have often said the same thing. I may say, if you have worries about money, please don't worry about it, come in. I have often said that if I feel it is really a concern about money because the person hasn't got money. But I usually say, I can't discuss it on the phone because it depends on many things, why don't you come in and don't worry about it.

Now answer me. I'm the prospective patient on the other line asking: Doctor, what is your fee?

*Candidate:* I'll tell you what I used to do.

*Greenson:* What would you do today?

*Candidate:* I tell them I would like them to come in for the first interview when we could discuss the matter more easily, and we would decide then on the basis of their financial status what the fee would be. . . .

*Do You Set the Initial Interview Fee Over the Phone?*

*Candidate:* . . . but I was trying to say that there was a time when I would have set the initial interview fee, and the subsequent fee would be decided later.

*Greenson:* Don't you feel there's a disadvantage to setting the initial interview fee?

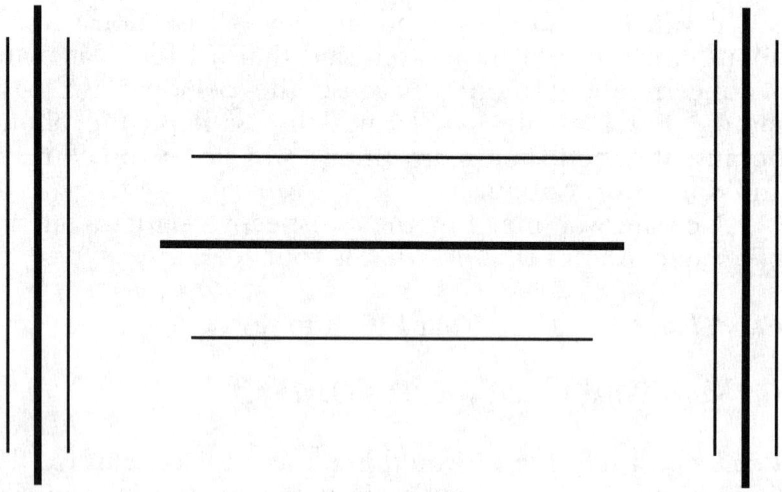

*Candidate:* Yes, I think so.

*Greenson:* There's also an advantage to it, incidentally. You get it out of the way once and for all if you said it. But the disadvantage is maybe it is an unfair fee, unfair to you, or to the patient. But there's something else in it that I don't like. It's not the idea that it may be fair or unfair, it's the idea that you are somehow a merchant, I can't get over that feeling, that this is saying okay, I'm for sale at such a price.

*Candidate:* You have to understand there are patients who are not acquainted with psychiatric fees and are used to this kind of approach.

*Greenson:* So you are saying, "that's your problem, Greenson." Well, I believe you're right.

*Candidate:* It is taught to them, they're told to ask . . .

*Greenson:* . . . what are the fees. I think I want to remind you of Freud's attitude about it. He said that doctors are so damned hypocritical. They pretend they're not in business. They're in business—I mean he doesn't say that—so they are interested in the fee. Why do they pretend they're not interested in the fee? Why are we so snobbish? Let's admit it. But I do have that prejudice, and I do resent the question. But I think it should be answered the way we just discussed. I also like to tell the patient, if you're really worried about money, please don't worry. Come in, and we'll decide. But in truth, I just don't like the question.

This seems like a good point for us to stop until next time.

---

February 24, 1959: Preliminary Interviews—Lecture II

---

*Greenson:* The last hour we started with preliminary interviews and I tried first of all to discuss the aims of the preliminary interviews, and I think we boiled it down to three main aims.

One major aim was the appraisal of the patient, and this we broke down into, well, the first thing we want to decide is do you have an emergency or don't you? Once you decide that you don't have an emergency, then you have the time to do a more definitive and careful appraisal. Then that definitive appraisal really consists of trying to assess the ego functions, the psychological mindedness of the patient, and the motivations of the patient, plus the external circumstances that are involved which may influence you. So that's the main aim: appraisal of the patient. Then we talked about two other aims. One is that the patient should get some therapeutic benefit from the interviews. And the third aim would be from our point of view, whether we want this patient, what do we want to do with this patient, do we want him.

The next thing we talked about last time was: How do we accomplish the appraisal of the patient? And here we talked about the fact that in the preliminary interviews we not only observe the patient, and listen to the history and the data that the patient has to tell us, but we try to facilitate the establishment of an object relationship with this patient, and we observe this process. I think that's what we covered the last time. This last point was what was new about initial or preliminary interviews, using the situation of the preliminary interview for trying to set up some kind of a relationship with the patient; in other words, not just being an observer, a recorder, and a history taker, but also participating somehow in this interview in order to set up an object relationship with the patient. Any questions about this? If not, let's go on. There's so much to cover. I don't want to dilly-dally with all kinds of unimportant ideas.

I want to talk about the technique of doing the initial interviews, but again I find myself having to say, before we get to the technique, there are a few things we ought to talk about. If you think of the initial interviews, and you think of your own experiences, what are the dangers of the preliminary interviews? What do you have to be careful about? What do you look for, what do you pay attention to? What do you keep in mind?

# 8 | What Can Trigger an Acute Psychotic Break?

I keep alert to three things: One, I want to be careful that the initial interviews do not stir up or precipitate an acute psychotic break in the patient. Now I know that sounds rather dramatic to put it this way, that the interviewer could do this, but it can be done. I've seen it. I've seen it in psychiatric candidates applying for training, who in the course of the initial interviews with the training analyst have gone right into an acute psychotic break, and who were not acutely psychotic until then. And it's not just here in LA that we have seen it; this has been recorded. Why? How can that be? Let's assume that we are not the worst therapists or the most crude people, how can it be that interviewing the patient could produce an acute psychotic break?

*Candidate:* I think if you're too passive with a patient who is teetering.

[41] Greenson makes this point clear elsewhere (1967). "Further-more, silence is one of the greatest stresses that our patients have to bear in the analytic situation, and should therefore be administered thoughtfully in quality and quantity. Silence is both a passive and an active intervention on the part of the analyst" (p. 374). In these remarks Greenson is talking about the need to be thoughtful about where and when one is silent in psychoanalytic treatment, where there has been some explanation of the behavior a patient can expect from the analyst. Silence in an initial contact is likely to be unexplained and therefore to be very stressful, potentially triggering a serious decompensation is an emotionally fragile patient.

[42] "Defense refers to processes which safeguard against danger and pain and is to be contrasted to instinctual activities which seek pleasure and discharge" (Greenson, 1967, p. 77). By probing, Greenson is talking about asking questions that may be very pertinent to the interviews, but might not be tolerable by certain fragile patients. Here he points to a potential danger in becoming too formulaic in one's approach to an evaluation, which includes the use of forms required by insurance companies that ask very probing questions. Since it is not possible to know ahead of time what questions a given patient might find too probing, Greenson will advise a slow uncovering of information rather than a lot of direct, penetrating questions.

## You Sit Silent Like a Mummy

*Greenson:* Well, I would certainly say if you're too passive, you're giving him too much stress. Pure and simple stress. I certainly would agree with you that in the initial interview in which you sit there silent as a mummy, it is a terrific amount of stress to impose on a patient.[41] That I agree, and that can trigger it. That would certainly be a poor way of conducting initial interviews. And that certainly does happen.

## You Probe and Fragile Defenses Weaken[42]

But what else can trigger it, in a so-called properly conducted initial interview? What would probing the patient, asking questions about a patient do to a patient's defense impulse balance? Let's say a patient is struggling against certain sexual impulses, it's nip and tuck whether he's maintaining his control over them. And now you come innocently and start asking him questions like, now what about masturbation, when did it begin? What kind of fantasies do you have? And he's been struggling against this by repression, by isolation, denial, God knows. Your questions interfere with these defenses, just your probing, conscious questions can interfere with the defenses, weaken them sufficiently that they just break. Again I'm supposing this is not altogether a healthy person, or it wouldn't happen, but in a really sick person, just the questioning and probing might do it.

## You Stir Up a Repressed Traumatic Event

Or take some traumatic event that a patient is struggling to maintain in repression, and you stir up a repressed traumatic event. You say, now what about the death of your father, when did it happen, how did you feel? Now this is associatively connected to all kinds of guilts. Here you go,

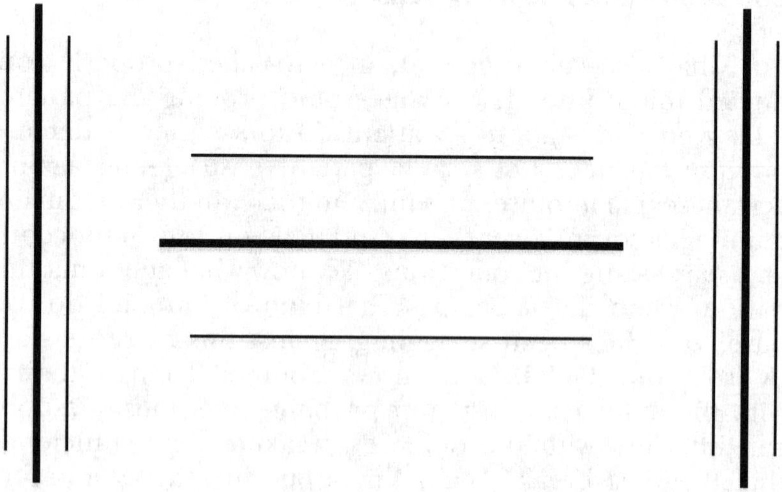

you mobilize this. So just the questioning can stir up and disturb the defenses. So I think the two points we have here are: Initial interview by probing disturbs defenses; or, by stressful silence, can really cause disturbances and precipitate a break in a patient who's teetering on the edge. This would be one of the dangers of putting the patient on the couch too early, which I have seen. I have seen quick appraisal of the patient in a half an hour, and because someone had said, I think this is an analytic patient, plunking the patient down on the couch, and bon voyage! There they went. They just drifted off. I saw this happen a few years ago with a very experienced analyst who saw this woman patient for approximately half an hour, and made then all the practical arrangements to begin analysis. The next hour the patient lay on the couch, and in the first hour on the couch she began to say, "What's wrong here," and, "Oh, I see how you feel about me, I know what you're thinking." He made a mental note about so much projection going on, then, in the second hour on the couch, he was pretty convinced she was psychotic. By the third hour he called for help, please what the hell do I do, this woman is acutely psychotic, which she has remained ever since.

Number one is the precipitating of the acute psychotic break. To me this is one of the biggest dangers that you have to keep in mind during initial interviews. And again I say, please don't trust anyone else's evaluation, I don't care how good they are, and how well studied, or whatever they have done, I don't care. I've seen excellent people slip or not see something, or I've seen it in myself, where a person was sent around to be interviewed by five, six, seven of us, and some of us missed. I have missed it myself. I remember seeing one man in initial interviews in which I put down: This man is either one of the greatest talents we ever had, or an impending schizophrenic break. Unfortunately the second one was correct. When he had two more interviews he was already in the psychosis. I listened to this man in the first hour, to his intuitiveness, his freedom, and I said, gee this is a great talent or a schizophrenic. Well, sometimes it's hard to know.

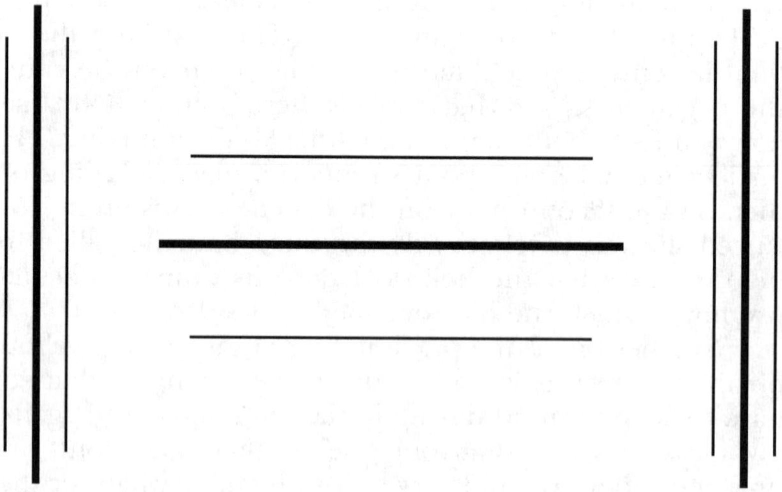

## Incipient Psychotic Breaks Outside Your Immediate Control

I'm sure other factors besides the questioning are harder to control than your thinking and your orientation and how you proceed; those are more under your control. But you know there are some things that you can't help. The way you sit during the interview may have a meaning for the patient that you can't anticipate. There are breaks that are already going on, that haven't been recognized. Here, in order to test out whether I'm seeing correctly the beginning of a break of some kind, I'll be rather careful, but I might add a little stress. Here's a situation where I might, for example, try to be a little silent just to see what happens, to put the patient under a little bit of stress. Again, I must feel pretty sure that I can gauge how bad a break this is, how manageable it is, in order to do it, but I would do certain things like this, just to make sure when I'm uncertain about it. At any rate, that's a whole category of dangers, incipient break, patient on the verge of an acute break, coming for preliminary interviews, and asking for help because of it. And we must recognize that many patients take this time to come and reach out for help.

# 9 Do Face-to-Face Interviews Complicate the Transference?

*Candidate:* How do people who advocate putting the patient on the couch as soon as possible, like in the second hour, how do they address this problem of an incipient psychosis?

*Greenson:* Their answer is, and this comes to the second kind of danger, their answer is it is crucial to avoid the danger in prolonged face-to-face interviews of interfering with the transference neurosis development. They feel, once they can ascertain quickly that the patient isn't overtly psychotic, or once someone else has ruled out that the patient is psychotic, fine. Well, I don't go for this. I think they justify it on the basis (and if you read Freud's paper "On Beginning the Treatment" [1913], one of the technical papers, he mentions very briefly the dangers of prolonged face-to-face interviews) that it interferes with the transference development.

[43] Since 1959, psychoanalytic theory has shifted further and further away from the idea that the analyst seeking an ideal of "anonymity" is either desirable or possible. Instead, there is an increasing appreciation that what has been called "anonymity" is more likely to be a way of relating that has an impact on the transference–countertransference mix, which of course is dependent on the qualities unique to every patient–therapist pair. Greenson's comments are made with reference to a more classical view of technique that goes back to the topographic period of Freud's theoretical ideas about the mind and analytic technique.

It's true, I think the danger of taking your time in interviewing the patient face-to-face is that you will complicate the transference development. After all, the less the patient knows about you, the more anonymous you are, the greater ease they have to develop a transference neurosis. In face-to-face meetings they are going to get certain glimpses of you, and you're going to lose some of your anonymity, and you're going to give a certain amount of transference gratification. It's going to interfere in some way, and the rationalization would be therefore that you should keep it to a minimum. But when you weigh the other dangers, I say, I would rather complicate the transference development than risk the psychosis. My reason for that is, if you are circumspect in the way you deal with the initial interviews none of the things you do is unanalyzable. So you sit face-to-face, and it's true the patient gets to see something about you in the way you talk or how you respond or whatever, and this will reduce your anonymity; but it's not unanalyzable.[43]

[44] In the passage that follows this statement, Greenson clarifies the difference between trying to empathize during initial interviews and empathy based on an established, ongoing treatment relationship. By contrast to efforts at empathy during the initial interviews, Greenson (1967) clearly feels that empathy is essential to analytic treatments: "It is necessary for the analyst to feel close enough to the patient to be able to empathize with the most intimate details of his emotional life; yet he must be able to become distant enough for dispassionate understanding" (p. 279).

In the same paragraph, he distinguishes between empathy and sympathy: "The analyst's sympathy or undue compassion, if revealed to the patient, might be perceived either as a transference reward or punishment." Greenson is pointing out that attempts at empathy in initial interviews are more based on who our patients remind us of than our experience with the patient, and for that reason such empathic responses are less reliable. Although Greenson does not go into it here, it seems reasonable to consider that such early experiences of empathy, when they prove over time to be incorrect, may be a useful resource for identifying potential countertransference blind spots.

# 10 | The Role of Empathy in the Initial Interviews

*Candidate:* I think the underlying issue with regard to when to put the patient on the couch, whether silence would be constructive, whether probing would be constructive, is the capacity of the analyst to empathize with this particular individual and his conflicts at this time. If the capacity for empathy is working well, then there will be sufficient respect for the individual's capacity to tolerate silence, or interventions of various sorts.

*Greenson:* I'll tell you doctor, the danger of empathy with a new patient is this: Empathy has to be based on your quick alignment of this patient to people who seem similar in your own experience. The more I know someone the better I empathize, the less I know him, the more I'm going on, who does he remind me of.[44] Now, it's true, that isn't nothing, that is not to be dismissed, but you cannot empathize with a totally strange person. The fact that you empathize at all means that in some way he's familiar. But he's familiar not

on the basis of the data that you are picking up now, but based on the people he reminds you of. In other words, if I wanted to empathize with you, I empathize with you because you remind me of x, and y, and z in other people. And this is relatively unreliable as compared to if I really got to know you over months and years of work. Now the danger with empathy in a new patient is that it's a kind of borrowed empathy. I am empathizing with him on the basis of models I'm constructing that he reminds me of, and that can be awfully wrong.

I agree that empathy does give you all kinds of important clues in terms of how much stress, how little stress, how much you can go on hunches and quick, intuitive assessments. I agree, but it's relatively unreliable as compared to knowing the patient and then empathizing with him. I have learned to be careful about my empathic judgments in the beginning of knowing the patient, because I just find they're unreliable. I have often been very right, penetratingly right, but I can also tell you that I have been so wrong, because they reminded me of someone, yet in certain very crucial ways they were different. And I didn't see it in the beginning. I think empathy in the initial interviews is necessary and helpful, but to be taken with many grains of salt, because you're empathizing and building models of a person whom you don't know. He may look like x, talk like y, sit like z, have a familiar face, and have a history that reminds you of patient so-and-so, but what it adds up to I think you have got to be careful about. So I think empathy is of value, but of limited value when you don't know a person.

# 11 | What Is Unique about the Initial Interviews?

*Greenson:* Let's go on: What determines the special character of the initial interviews?

*Candidate:* The way the patient behaves in the interview.

*Greenson:* Of course, but let's not be so obvious. I'm asking you special questions. Here, for example, is what I mean.

## Two Strangers Are Meeting

*Greenson:* How a person reacts to strangers will be a very crucial determinant of the initial interview situation, because what is unique or special about an initial interview is that a patient is going to meet a doctor he doesn't know. Similarly, given x number of analysts, what determines the way they handle it? How do you react to strangers? The point is that it's a very special situation because two strangers are

[45] It seems worth highlighting here that Greenson is saying no matter how therapists are taught to do their work, the way they act will in part be determined by their personalities. He recognizes his own limitations as a role model. In particular, he is emphasizing the need to know your own habitual ways of reacting to strangers, and to appreciate the impact these factors will have on the atmosphere of the initial interviews.

[46] Since this was said in 1959, it seems worth noting the fact that general transference attitudes toward doctors have changed in the last forty years, along with a change in the way many doctors practice. For example, it was common in 1959 for the family doctor to make house visits, which is now no longer common and perhaps even rare. Beepers were unique to the doctor on call, whereas now they are used by nearly everyone. In general, doctors are less idealized, to a point where patients may even come to a doctor not expecting to find someone who cares. There even may be an initially negative expectation. The point here is to appreciate that the doctor's place in our society has changed over the past forty years, changing the attitudes that patients bring to the initial meeting.

meeting. You know there are certain patients or people who even though they are phobic or this or that, when they meet strangers they act in a certain way; or there are analysts, no matter how well analyzed they are, when it comes to meeting strangers, they react in a certain way. I can talk to you until I'm blue in the face about how to conduct initial interviews, but how you will do it will in great part be determined by how you meet strangers. You know that all my talking, and coaxing, and pleading, and yelling does not alter the fact that how you meet strangers will have an effect on how you open the door, how you say hello, how you sit down.[45] That's what I mean, certain special factors that influence the character or the color of the initial interview situation. What else? Any other special factors that might play a special role in initial interviews?

### Preconceived Ideas the Patient Has about the Doctor

*Candidate:* The preconceived ideas the patient has about the doctor.

*Greenson:* Right! The special transference that you represent to a patient going to a doctor. The whole business of being a doctor or being an analyst. The patient will have preconceived notions no matter how you may be, or what's wrong with them, it will influence it, right. What else?

*Candidate:* Patients expecting the doctor to be the savior, omnipotent.[46]

*Greenson:* Right.

### Preconceived Ideas the Doctor Has about the Patient

*Greenson:* But I am thinking of the doctor's expectation. What the patient represents in terms of the patient's social setting. In other words, the preconceived ideas the doctor

has about the patient. How you react to sick people who are desperate. How you react to whatever particular transference figure the patient represents to you. I think you can see how you will react quite differently if the patient is a Catholic, or if the patient is very rich, or if the patient is very poor, or if the patient is a Negro. This has not to do with the specific qualities of the patient but the transference that the patient stirs up in you, and it will certainly influence the way you handle the initial interviews. What else?

*Candidate:* The symptomatology of the patient, perhaps you react differently to a phobic than to a depressed patient.

*Greenson:* These are all transference provoking qualities which may be present in you or in the patient, which you can't predict. You may react some way because the patient is red headed. There's something else I'm after, though, which I think plays a particular role in the initial interviews. Not only in initial interviews, but also in subsequent meetings.

## How the Patient Is Referred to You

*Candidate:* I don't know if this is what you're thinking of, but, how the patient is referred to you has set your mind in a certain way. The patient who got your name out of the phone book is automatically and unconsciously handled differently from someone who is referred by Anna Freud.

*Greenson:* I think that's a good point. I think that's absolutely right. It's not only what qualities the patient has but your reaction to the source of referral that can play a big role. My God, I remember when I was a beginner, the first time I was sent a patient by a prominent analyst I promptly botched it up. I was so eager to do it right. I'm sure that's happened to you, well, maybe you won't admit it, but it's happened to me. In fact, this is one of the reasons why it's

not a good idea, in fact it is contraindicated to send patients to candidates in treatment with you. What else?

*Candidate:* What about your own freshness or fatigue when you see the patient.

*Greenson:* That's more general.

## The Special Role of Exhibitionism and Voyeurism

*Greenson:* I am thinking about the special role of exhibitionism and voyeurism in the initial interview situation. Here is a situation where you are on view. You know the patient is looking, the patient is sort of shopping, sizing you up, so you're conscious of being looked at. Also the patient knows you are looking. You are assessing them, sizing them up. You're going to say I will see you or I won't; I can help you or I can't help you. So it's loaded with this whole question of revealing versus hiding, looking and being looked at. I think that your particular difficulties or ease in such situations play a role. There are people who have great difficulties with this, but there are other people who like it and are good at it. I think that's more or less what I had in mind about the special determinants: meeting strangers, transference reactions to the patient, special transference provoking qualities in the patient and the analyst, exhibitionism and voyeurism, all of which affect the way you conduct the initial interviews. I should, I suppose, add the source of referrals.

# 12

## How to Conduct the Initial Interviews

**Facilitating the Establishment of an Object Relationship**

*Greenson:* Now let's talk about the technique, how you really conduct the initial interviews. To go back, we said our aim is to facilitate the establishment of an object relationship, that this is the very special thing we want in addition to observing the patient and listening to the patient. So, the question is, how do you go about facilitating the establishment of an object relationship? I know this is a tremendous question. I don't think we're going to answer it completely, but by God, I'm determined we answer it substantially. How do you go about trying to facilitate a situation which is conducive for the patient to establish an object relationship with you?

*Candidate:* You have to make yourself inviting, so you are something good to eat.

[47] I think an anecdote may help highlight an important issue that is raised here. Early on in my adult psychoanalytic training, one of my supervisors wrote in a report: "Dr. Jaffe shows great promise to become an excellent analyst, particularly as he becomes less concerned with being so helpful." My supervisor referred to being "helpful" here to comment on my desire to promote relief in my analysand, which can interfere with analytic progress. In the midst of an analysis, as compared to initial interviews, it is crucial that the analyst be tolerant of the patient's distress in the service of exploration, rather than attempting to bring relief as soon as possible.

By contrast, Greenson is referring to the importance of conveying the desire to help a patient during the initial contacts. As he has already said, creating an atmosphere where the patient feels you want to help promotes the establishment of a relationship, and that in turn facilitates the evaluation. He is more concerned that the doctor's desire to help not be suppressed during the initial interviews, than with the idea that the doctor should feign a desire to be helpful. In the course of these lectures, Greenson makes it clear that he felt the desire to help should be automatic for doctors, or they are in the wrong line of work.

*Greenson:* I think that's pretty good. But you're talking at a deeper level than I'm willing to go at the moment. Before the patient will eat us, let's go a little less deeply into it, because you're saying it on the most regressive terms. There's something true in what you say, and it would certainly be true of very sick patients.

## Establish Yourself as Someone Who Wants to Help

*Candidate:* I think you have to establish yourself as someone who wants to help.

*Greenson:* You want to present yourself as someone who wants to help.[47] That's correct. Why should being someone who wants to help facilitate the establishment of an object relationship?

*Candidate:* That's presumably why they're coming to see you, they want help. They are suffering from some stress or pain. If you conduct it in such a way that they feel you're bored or not interested, that's against the whole idea of why the patient is coming to see you. Then they wouldn't want to establish a relationship.

*Greenson:* I would certainly say that that's part of what I'd try to get across to my patient. How would you do it?

*Candidate:* I would answer the question this way. You present yourself, you contact the patient, you react to him, and facilitate a dialogue.

*Greenson:* You present yourself to the patient, you contact him, and react to him. I think that's good. I just think you're saying it too quickly. I would like to elaborate upon it because you present yourself to him and you react to him in a certain way in order to make yourself accessible for contact with him. How I would like to present it is this way: I like to create a certain atmosphere, in fact we all do. We have

[48] These issues are important even for therapists who work in institutional settings where they do not decorate their offices, and in many cases the offices are not warm, welcoming, or particularly comfortable. The setting is still affecting the patient's reaction to the initial interviews. In institutional settings, whatever can be offered by way of helping a patient to feel more comfortable may be even more important to establishing a relationship. Institutional settings tend to lead patients to feel they are "just" one of many rather than an individual. Of course, some of the elements Greenson describes as part of this facilitative atmosphere can be done anywhere: showing interest and respect, paying attention, listening carefully, and being responsive.

[49] In what follows here, Greenson makes a distinction between functioning therapeutically versus analytically, functioning as a psychoanalyst versus functioning as a psychotherapist. What's more, he says that the identity of the therapist is different from that of the analyst, whether the therapist is analytically trained or not. He does not see these differences so much as conscious roles but as differing identities. Greenson clearly felt that both identities are important for the analyst, who must rely more on the psychotherapist identity during the initial interviews.

There are several important considerations raised here. One, with the increase of managed care, psychotherapists are being asked to incorporate more and more procedures into their initial interviews for verification of "medical necessity." Since the managed care procedures may or may not be consistent with a given psychotherapist's way of conducting initial interviews, there is a risk that these procedures interfere with the therapist's psychotherapist identity. In such cases, it is important that psychotherapists find ways to prevent the managed care procedures from disrupting their psychotherapist identity. One way to do so might be to clarify in the initial interviews what is being done for insurance requirements (the financial interests of the patient) versus what is being done in the best interests of the patient's mental health. This will be particularly important in those cases where protecting the patient's access to treatment (i.e., getting treatment paid for) may conflict with the patient's best interests psychologically.

Consider the following case in point, one which does arise often for analytic psychotherapists who work with managed care companies. Due to managed care policies, it may be necessary to see a patient less frequently than is optimal from a psychoanalytic, diagnostic viewpoint. The patient cannot afford more frequent sessions or sessions for a longer period of time than the managed care company deems necessary, or the psychotherapist is not permitted to make any treatment arrangements outside the managed care system, even if the patient can afford it and wishes to do so. These realities need to be clarified as part of the initial interviews or the psychotherapeutic identity of the therapist has been compromised. Once clarified, however, the patient will have a sense of the therapist's integrity and true wish to be helpful. Greenson clearly sees these elements as essential to the initial interviews.

it already in the way we have our waiting rooms set up, and the way we have our treatment rooms set up, we are already creating a certain atmosphere. Some of the things we do to facilitate an object relation have to do with this atmosphere, that we have already set up. I think when I go out and say, I'm Dr. Greenson, you must be so-and-so, that's all part of creating an atmosphere. I think my introducing myself, my saying, have a seat, showing him two seats so he can pick one, my offering him a cigarette, I think this is all part of an atmosphere, just like the drapes in my office, or the pictures in my office, or the color of my walls, are part of the atmosphere.[48]

I show him my interest and my respect. I pay attention to what he says, and listen carefully. You know all these things are making myself accessible as an object, trustworthy as an object, and appetizing as an object, so that he is willing to let out some of his feelings toward me. I think it's important to permit the patient to see some responsiveness; not deadpan, not boredom, not merely detective work, but to see a response in you. To permit the patient to see your responses to some degree is part of saying: I'm human, I have feelings, and I have empathy. Now again you must modulate this, you can't let it get to such a point that your responses influence the patient too much, you must be careful that they don't traumatize the patient. I would certainly not advise you to weep when the patient tells you something sad, or to jump with fright, but to show certain degrees of emotional response in your face, by all means.

I don't want to give the impression of manipulating the patient. I want to say that in the initial interview situation we are faced with the problem of making sure our patient gets to see a genuine part of the therapeutic identity, not of the analytic identity.[49] Now I don't know if that's helpful to you to make a difference there, but this is what I mean. I want to make sure my patient gets to see certain parts of me that ordinarily I don't expose to my patients. In my everyday analytical work they don't get to see it, they are not particularly aware I'm a doctor, they are not particularly aware that I'm respectful, it's taken for granted in the way

[50] Greenson is referring to the fact that his experience of others is determined in part by the context of the meeting. Meeting a stranger in an initial interview calls forth different aspects of his identity than meeting someone for the first time at a party. He wants to emphasize that the psychotherapist identity is authentic and special, but it is not a role the psychotherapist consciously plays to manipulate patients, any more than the role of son, daughter, father, mother, wife, or husband are manipulations. He is clarifying that his psychotherapist identity differs from his psychoanalyst identity (which refers to that identity he has developed related to the analytic process), which would not be appropriate to the initial interview. Thus, when he acts to alleviate suffering as a psychotherapist in an initial interview, he relies on a different identity from when he acts in a manner that increases the suffering in a patient undergoing psychoanalysis.

[51] Greenson (1967) clarifies that by manipulation he means, "an evocative activity undertaken by the therapist without the knowledge of the patient" (p. 50). He goes on to give an example where the therapist might be silent to let the strength of an affect grow in order to make it more demonstrable to the patient. He makes it clear, however, that "the deliberate and conscious assumption of roles or attitudes is anti-analytic since it creates an unanalyzable situation. There is an element of deception and trickery which eventuates in a realistic mistrust of the therapist." At the same time he admits such procedures may be necessary in certain psychotherapeutic situations. At the same time, he recognized that there were opposing views to the ones he expresses here (Bacon et al., 1946).

that I'm aware of what's going on. Here's a new patient, a frightened patient, one reaching out for help, one full of prejudice, anxieties, and depressions. I don't want to manipulate him. I want to let out something that I genuinely feel. These are people who need some help, and I want them to see that I'm seriously interested in trying to help them.

*Candidate:* I think that when a patient comes to see you, you don't have to facilitate anything, they will respond to you anyway. That is, you don't do anything special. You may respond very differently to different people, but I don't think you do something to make them see you. You're talking about it as though you do something special, but I don't think you do.

*Greenson:* I think you are wrong. Let me tell you something. Some people that I saw in my office, let's say that I see them at a social gathering. I would not react the same way at all, not at all. The fact that they're in my office, already does something to me, not consciously, but the fact that they're in my office makes a big difference. I would permit certain prejudices in a social setting, for example, which I do not permit to happen to me in my office. I cathect the fact that they are patients, that they're in trouble, and how I pay attention to them. I think I'm much more tolerant, at least I hope I'm much more tolerant in my office than I am socially.[50]

*Candidate:* It sounds like playing a role.

*Greenson:* You see by calling it playing a role you make it much more like a conscious, manipulative thing.[51]

*Candidate:* I don't mean that it's conscious.

*Your Psychotherapeutic Identity versus Analytic Identity*

*Greenson:* What I do is I permit a certain aspect of my therapeutic identity, my identity as a doctor-therapist to come out

in this situation, which I think is conducive to the patient so that he will relate to me. And these consist of the various things that many of you have mentioned. Let me just rattle some of them off. The patient is sick and I'm a doctor. I'm serious in wanting to help and I'm interested. I respect what he's saying. I respect his misery. I permit myself to be somewhat responsive. I'm not a deadpan, I'm rather open in my reactions. I'm rather forthright without being blunt and without being tactless. If he says something, I will pursue it. I consider it a professional situation, and I'm very professional. It's not social. It's serious without being morbid, but it isn't flippant either. You know, I don't want to be wisecracking, and I'm not wisecracking. It's serious.

I said I introduced myself, I tell the patient what I know about him. I offer him a cigarette because I usually take one myself, and then I look at the patient expectantly, I try not to say anything, I just sort of look at him. Now sometimes he doesn't take that cue, and then I'll say something very noncommittal like, "Yes?" to see what he does with that. In other words, I try not to intrude my personality into the situation. I will listen to him responsively, not without reaction, but with a certain amount of responsiveness. Warmly I call it, warm listening, but I will be careful to avoid all kinds of condemnatory responses. Not to go tsk, tsk, in my face or in my gestures. I try to be natural in my analytic identity. I should really say, I think, psychotherapeutic identity, more correctly, because I think in this situation I'm a psychotherapist rather than an analyst, but an analytically trained psychotherapist. Does that make it clearer?

*Candidate:* In a sense, I guess you're right, the psychotherapeutic stance does facilitate something. Without all these things being done that you have described to create an atmosphere, something will happen in the relationship that you don't want to happen, there will be some anxiety or fear as a response to you. That naturalness in your therapeutic voice is crucial.

*Greenson:* Let's say, I try to create an atmosphere in which the patient will try to establish contact. Now of course he's

[52] More and more, the meaning of analytic anonymity (abstinence) to the patient is being questioned. Originally it came along with Freud's topographic theories of the mind, and his early (topographic) ideas about the causes of symptoms, the nature of intrapsychic conflict, and the resulting psychoanalytic technique. The analyst was to be a blank screen for the projection of the patient's inner world. Unfortunately, as Freud updated his theories of the mind, he did not go back over his papers on the theory of technique and revise them. Fortunately, many contemporary analysts have considered how to make modern technique fit with modern theory, and a view has emerged in which the analyst can never be completely uninvolved and anonymous. Greenson seems to recognize this as he speaks of being "relatively anonymous." Even with these changes over time in analytic thought, however, you are unlikely to see an analyst with pictures of his or her children in the office, as I noticed when I visited the office of a colleague who does hypnosis.

going to distort it in his own way or try to change it. It's not easy for some people to establish contact, particularly people who have problems revealing themselves and meeting strangers. What's more, your own particular needs and anxieties will influence this atmosphere and interfere with it.

*Candidate:* I wonder if the word *appropriate* can be used in there some way, that one permits oneself to show some appropriate behavior. If something is humorous, you can smile, if there is a very traumatic event, you can show a reaction to that. Not to a marked degree, but appropriate.

*Greenson:* I permit myself an appropriate quality or quantity of response. By appropriate I mean psychotherapeutically appropriate. Here's an example of a patient with a horrendous thing that happened; a baby drowned when a year old. I know if she would tell me this I would, just like now, I would have a pained look on my face. I would feel that way and I would show it. I might wince. I know it is very helpful to my patient that I would allow myself this reaction. Again let's not exaggerate and say that this is curative to the patient, but it is crucial to be natural in your psychotherapeutic identity. I call it the *identity* because I do think it has to do with identity. Again I think it's part of the problem of analysts doing initial interviews compared to psychotherapists who don't have all of the restrictions we analysts always keep in mind, of not responding to our patients, or being relatively anonymous.[52] I'm sure that some analysts might disagree with some of this, other analysts may agree, but this is my way of working, and I think it is correct.

## What if the Patient Does Not Talk?

*Greenson:* But what happens when you look at the patient, and you look quizzically and you say, "Yes?" You wait a short time and add, "What about telling me something about yourself," and the patient can't. You know this happens. The patient comes in and looks at you, you look at them,

[53] Greenson's ideas here are applicable whatever the treatment modalities of the interviewer, be they medication, analytic therapies, cognitive–behavioral therapies, or others. It is not possible to evaluate a patient who won't talk to you, making it necessary to try and address the transference meaning of the silence. Therapists who conduct initial interviews and can address such transference situations successfully will obviously have the ability to work with a wider range of patients, no matter what the modality of assessment and/or treatment.

you give them a cigarette, fine and great. Your therapeutic identity is showing all over, and the patient is still quiet. It happens. What do you do?

*Candidate:* I think you use a minimum of activity.

*Greenson:* All right, you've used it, and the patient is saying nothing.

*Candidate:* I think you finally have to get to the point and say I know something is bothering you, that's why you came, tell me what it is.

*Greenson:* And the patient still says, "Gee, I don't know, I can't talk." I'm a tough patient, come on now. Seriously, what happens if the patient looks and stammers and stutters and can't speak. Then you must make his inability to talk the subject of the talk. So you say to him, you seem to have trouble speaking. Tell me, do you always have such trouble, or is it only with me? You make this inability to speak a communicative subject, just as you do in an analytic hour, but somewhat differently. Since you don't know exactly what the anxiety is you don't call it anxiety, you just say, you seem to have difficulty. You make this resistance the subject of the talk. Very naturally, and again with respect, not critically, not reproachfully, but out of curiosity. You seem to have trouble in talking, how come? Do you always have it? Then the patient very often will start the talk and say, "Yes, I do." He tells you he has difficulty when he has to meet people who are doctors, or men, or older people, or people with mustaches. Or he will tell you, "I once had a terrible experience with a doctor." This is when the special transferences will come out.[53]

## What About Silence on the Part of the Interviewer?

I think it's worth talking about your silence and what it does to the patient. Earlier I said that I think one of the most

[54] Even though none of the candidates chooses to take up Greenson's challenge, there are instances where the more disturbed patient may not find silence stressful. Keep in mind that Greenson is talking about "silence on the part of the interviewer" not complete silence in the room. In fact, there are cases where sicker patients respond better to the more silent interviewer. For example, the paranoid patient can wish to fill the interview with information rather than be involved with the interviewer, such that attempts to be more involved on the part of the "helpful" interviewer can trigger homosexual anxieties and disruptive regression.

stressful things you can do to a patient in an initial interview is to keep quiet. Now as long as the patient is talking, that's not too much of a stress, as long as you're responsive with your affect, your look, or with your posture in some way. But even so, after a while your silence is a kind of stress for the patient, it can even be felt as an oppression. It can have all kinds of meanings you don't know. You don't know what it means to the patient, but be aware that silence is a stress for the patient, particularly early in the initial interview situation. The little responses, verbal responses, of yes or no, or aha, little things like this, which are not really anything except part of what I call the natural responsiveness, are helpful to the patient. Of course you may want to deliberately cause some stress to the patient at one point or another in the interview. So you may deliberately keep silent to see how the patient reacts to the silence. But I would caution you not to do that too early. Wait till you get to know the patient a little bit, and the patient gets to see your human qualities a bit, then you can do it toward the end of the initial interviews.

The more silence, the more stress. The more disturbed the patient therefore, the less silent I am. Would you agree with this formulation?[54] That the more disturbed, the sicker, the more psychotic, the more borderline the patient, the less I'm going to be silent. The more acute the break seems to be, if it's an acute break, or completely psychotic, or overwhelming anxiety, the more I'm going to structure the interview. Silence makes for unstructuredness, permitting the patient to do a rambling kind of free associative talk. Questioning is reassuring. It limits what the patient can say.

## What if You See the Patient Get Anxious?

*Greenson:* Now, let us say that as you are working along with the patient, you noticed the patient has some anxiety. As it happens, the patient starts to get ill at ease, you can see this. They are slurring over something, they seem ill at ease, tense, restless, disconcerted, harassed. What about this? What do you do with this?

[55] Here Greenson demonstrates the special place that anxiety holds in psychoanalytic theories of the mind. Diagnosis of a patient's inner psychological structure is highly related to learning how anxiety is experienced and managed. Does it function as a signal of meaningful information that leads to an adaptive response on the part of the patient? Does the anxiety overwhelm the patient and lead to maladaptive or traumatic responses? Greenson is drawing on the basic signal theory of affects that Freud developed with the structural model of the mind (Freud, 1923).

*Candidate:* You want to know what the patient is talking about at the time when he shows this anxiety.

*Greenson:* You're ahead of me there. You see, you're already trying to connect the anxiety to some content, which is I think correct, but that's not the first thing I think of. I don't think it's the first thing you think of.

*Candidate:* The reason I follow that bend is because you say the patient has been talking a while, seemed to be at ease, and then he becomes anxious. So one would wonder what suddenly occurred to make the patient anxious.

*Greenson:* I don't want to say you're wrong, I just don't think it is in order of what comes to my mind. True, I would think, what is it? But I would like to pay very special attention to the anxiety. I have certain thoughts about anxiety, I don't know what you think about when you see anxiety coming up in a patient, I don't know how you think about it.

*Candidate:* The first thought that comes to me is, I wonder if the patient himself recognizes his state. That he is restless. I just wonder and mention this, that he seems to be nervous. I want to see if he realizes that he is nervous. And if he says, yes, I am, well then you might say, well, do you know what it's connected to?

*Greenson:* That is more what causes my feelings too. That if I know that the patient is anxious, one of the things I want to know is what kind of a patient have I got? Have I got just a neurotic, have I got a hysteric, have I got a psychotic, have I got a borderline?[55] One of the places where I'm going to find out is right here. So if he's anxious, one of the things I can do is say, you seem a little nervous, or you seem to be bothered now. Is he aware of it? Is he not? Does he make some appropriate response, or an inappropriate response? Is it bizarre? I want to utilize his anxiety, or my awareness of his anxiety to confront him with it. I want to find out (1) is he aware, and (2) is he appropriately aware, because this

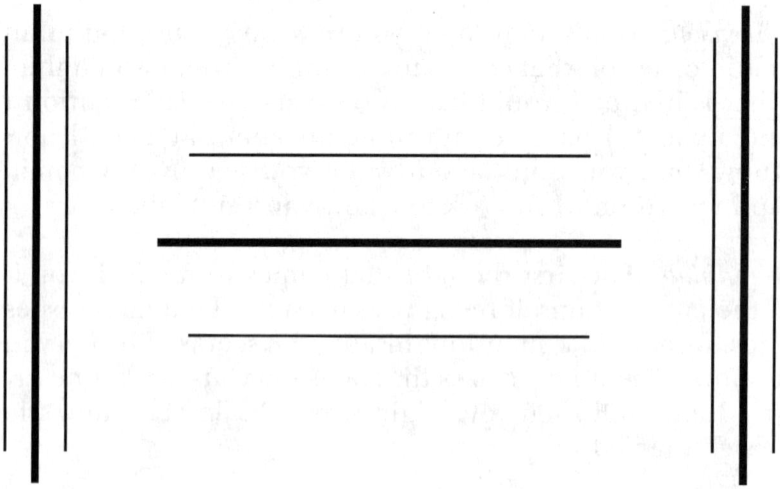

helps me to determine if this is a neurotic or borderline psychotic or whatever. I also make a mental note about what might be causing the anxiety, but that's not my primary concern at the moment.

*Candidate:* Also asking about the anxiety is establishing communication with the patient.

*Greenson:* Yes. It's important in terms of establishing empathy. When I notice it, and I mention it, and I let him talk to me about it, we're establishing a therapeutic relationship. Just with this. The same would go if he got depressed, if I saw him get tears in his eyes. I would say the same thing, you seem sad about this. In general for any affect that would come up, I would do the same thing, I would mention it to him and see, does he recognize it and does he recognize it appropriately, inappropriately, or bizarrely.

*Candidate:* How is this therapeutic?

*Greenson:* Here again I want to say something about what we talked about the last time, because the fact that you are confronting the patient does not frighten him necessarily. Quite the contrary, most patients will be reassured, whereas if you avoid confrontation, and try to help him change the subject you can really frighten him. There are instances where caution on your part, obvious caution, frightens your patient, and boldness or forthrightness is reassuring to the patient. We talked about this the last time, when I noticed a patient getting ill at ease about whether or not he was going to lie down on the couch, and I confronted him directly. My confronting him reassured him.

I certainly have seen a patient in anxiety, and I have said, well that's enough talking about this, now I want you to tell me, what about your job, where do you work? You can see a change in the patient. I'm sure you've all seen this kind of thing happening, and you say, enough, enough about this, let's go on to something else. With very sick patients I have done it, but I have also had very sick patients do it to me.

[56] Greenson (1967, pp. 307–308, 311–315) distinguishes between asking "relatively soft questions" during the initial interviews and asking more penetrating questions during analytic treatment. In fact, he makes it clear that during the treatment process, asking about details is crucial to confront and clarify the issues that arise.

[57] In what follows, Greenson will comment on assessing a number of ego functions, but he does not list them. He will focus on the following ego functions: object relations, defense mechanisms, self-concept, intelligence, affect organization, the defense–impulse balance, the interests of the patient, accomplishments, the quantity and quality of anxiety and depressiveness, the extent to which the sickness has invaded the total personality, the capacity to be creative, the length of time the patient has been struggling, and the libidinal organization. While Greenson initially says he will cover 12 ego functions, he agrees with a candidate who raised *self-concept* as another. For clarity's sake I have italicized the thirteen ego functions that are discussed.

It's very wise to listen to them, at least in the beginning, until you're sure. The point is that the less structure, the more you let them carry the ball, the more you will get to see about the patient. You don't have to do a mental status to find out if the patient is oriented in time. You can find out as much and more if you just let the patient ramble on. I listen to the data the patient is telling. And I also above all listen to how he tells it to me.

## How to Ask Questions in the Initial Interviews

Incidentally, I want to make a point about asking questions. I ask questions, but I generally ask questions in a way that permits the patient a chance to evade them. I think this is an important point. I don't ask sharp, pointed, specific questions. I ask rather blunt, soft questions, that he can push away. For example, let us say, the patient has told me about his symptoms, I will say, what about your family? I don't say, what about your mother and father, or what about your wife? I want to see what he calls his family, you know. Or I will say, what about sex? Again, I don't say, what about your present sex life, what about your childhood, what about masturbation? I know he can run, if I put it so generally, but I don't only want to see what he is willing to communicate, I also want to see what he doesn't want to communicate. I want both. And therefore, I use the relatively soft questions. Again, this is part of the preliminary interviews. Later on, if I want to sharpen this more, I can ask him more specific questions, but my first interventions, or my first questions, are rather soft ones.[56] All right.

## Appraising the Patient's Ego Functioning[57]

Now let's get back to our main outline, where I say, what we want to do is appraise our patient's ego functions. Now, what does that really mean? How do you appraise the ego's functioning? Everybody agrees that's the main thing we

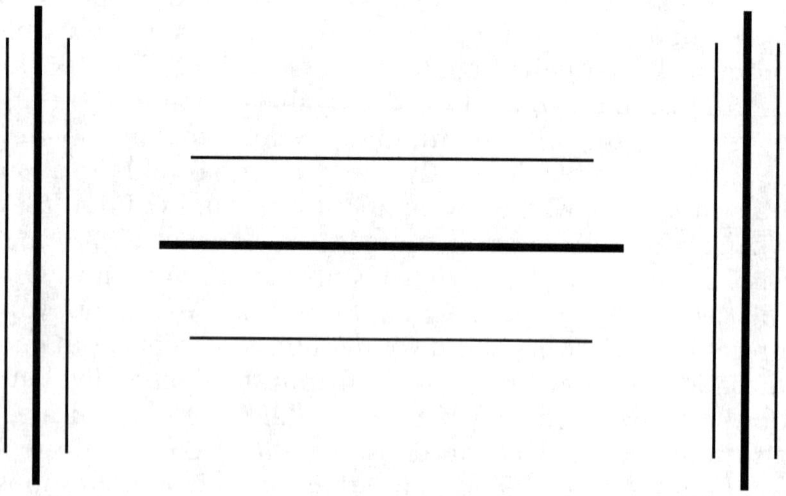

want to do, appraise the patient's ego functions. That's going to tell us how sick he is, how well he is, how treatable, analytic, nonanalytic. How do you appraise ego functions? I have listed down here twelve things that go under appraisal of ego functions in a patient. These are not all the ego functions, because there are many I haven't listed, but the ones that are important to check in the initial interview situation.

First of all is the whole business of the patient's contact, the *object relations*. Is the patient in contact with you? How does he relate to you? Does he relate to you? Does he relate appropriately to you? With affect, without, appropriate affect, not appropriate affect? You want to listen about his friends, his wife, what kind of things does he seem to say, does he really seem to be related to people, what kind of object relations?

In what other ways do you appraise ego functioning? What do you look for? Think of the initial interview, and think of what you listen for, in addition to the historical data, the data about the illness, what else do you listen for?

*Candidate:* You are also interested in the *defensive mechanisms*.

*Greenson:* Yeah, but that by God, I put way down at the bottom. I don't look at that in the beginning. That's not my main thing. Come on, think clinically as you really do. What do you look for?

*Candidate: Self-concept.*

*Greenson:* Concept of the self. I haven't thought of it but now that you mention it, I certainly think one should think of this, his conception of himself.

*Candidate:* One thing I like to know is intelligence; you might call it an intrinsic capacity. I like to know how intelligent he is and how he is able to think.

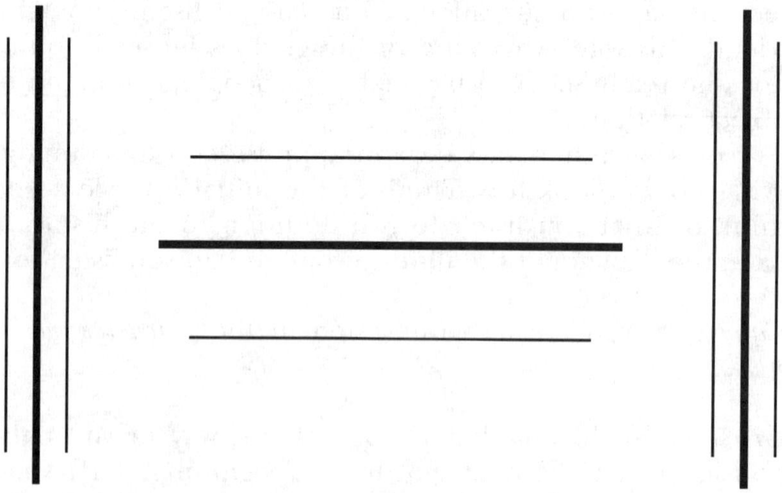

*Greenson:* Yes, *intelligence,* but is it a kind of effective intelligence? It is not only his I.Q. but his effective intelligence you want to know. I agree with you, that's part of the ego's functioning. What else?

*Candidate:* Psychological mindedness.

*Greenson:* That's a whole other category and I want to deal with that separately, because that's another category we want to go into. What else?

*Candidate:* Vocational adjustment, let's say, how he does on the job?

*Greenson:* Yeah, that's important, but not as a basic ego function. What is fundamental is *affects.* Is he affective, is he keenly affective, mildly affective, is it dampened, is it blunt, is it acute, is it appropriate, it is inappropriate, is it bizarre? Don't you look for that? I always do. What a difference if you see a guy with some expression, or a guy that's overacting all the time, or a guy that's got a blank look, or a guy with bizarre, peculiar affect. I do agree that one of the most important keys in terms of neurosis–psychosis prediction is his work history, his intellectual accomplishments.

What else? The balance between defense and control. Not just the kind of defenses, that's true, too, you want to look at them. But how good is the *defense–impulse balance?* A guy who starts telling you that suddenly he has become an actor outer, suddenly he has become promiscuous, suddenly he's become a drinker, uh oh, these are rather ominous indications of an upset in the balance between defenses and control.

What else? The *interests* of the patient, his cultural pursuits. Is he interested in music? Is he interested in art? Is he interested in hobbies, sports? God knows, I'm sure you are interested in his *accomplishments.* Not only do you want to know how sick this joker is, but what does he do despite his sickness? Was he ever a success, did he graduate from high school, college, make money, did he not make money, was

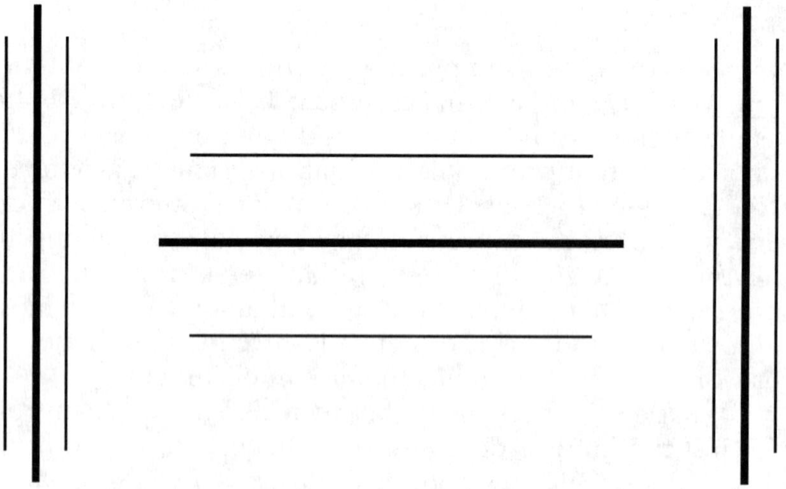

he a failure, does he have women? All of this. Not only am I interested in does he have anxiety, but what kind of anxiety, what are the things that frighten him, what is the quality of anxiety. Not only is he depressed, but the kind, the quality of the depression. If a man says, well I get moody, or a guy says, well, I get empty, I feel I'm not here. You know it's quite another thing if he says, I'm afraid people won't like me, and another thing if he says, well, I have a feeling people go around smelling me. You admit there's a difference. So it's not just the quantity, but the quality of the *anxiety,* and the quality of the *depressiveness* that you pay heed to, in terms of assessing his ego functions.

Now I bring up the kind of defenses. I certainly want to think of this, too. You know that projection, incorporation, introjection, and certainly denial are generally more serious than others. The kinds of symptoms also tell you something about the patient, and the kinds of thoughts that come up. How rigid is this man, how influenceable? Don't you look for rigidity in your preliminary interviews, before you decide what treatment to use?

*Candidate:* Rigidity relates to psychological mindedness too?

*Greenson:* In a way it can be related, but it doesn't have to be. A man could be psychologically minded and still be rigid, I think, but I think these are the kinds of things you look for. *How much has his sickness invaded the total personality?* This is part of the difficulty in doing initial interviews with adolescents who haven't found any identity and haven't done anything; it's so hard to evaluate these aspects of ego functioning.

*Candidate:* An accomplishment can be a sublimation or a reaction formation.

*Greenson:* Doctor, permit me to not accept this. It is academic, and I don't look at it that way. I'm not particularly interested in whether a man has become a champion bridge player due to a sublimation or a reaction formation.

*Candidate:* Isn't there a question about the nature of an accomplishment.

*Greenson:* Yes, but it's so hard to determine if it's a sublimation or a neutralized activity or a reaction formation, that's my point. Can you determine this by talking to a man in an initial interview? I don't know if I can. So I will put it down in terms of his accomplishments and his interests, but I would be unwilling to decide whether this is a sublimation or a neutralized function of his without knowing the man a long time. But, again, aren't we sort of quibbling, we both know what we mean and we both look for the same things.

*Candidate:* I was thinking of motivation.

*Greenson:* That's another chapter we will discuss, with both psychological mindedness and motivation as separate headings.

*Candidate:* Talents. Would that come under accomplishments?

*Greenson:* Talents. By all means. That should be under accomplishments; interests and talents, I know that given a choice, I'd always like to take a talented patient.

*Candidate:* There is also a question of the patient's capacity to be *creative.*

*Greenson:* Well, I think so too. I don't know if this is a prejudiced view, but I think that the whole procedure of being analyzed has an important creative aspect. The way you work with the patient, the way he produces the material from which you both construct and create something.

*Candidate:* You mention that you want to see how much of the personality is taken over by the symptomatology, but how about the freshness of a man who has done fairly well and then suddenly becomes upset, as opposed to a man who is chronically ill? What about cases when the ego has functioned fairly well until something came up?

[58] Gill's work focused more on the transference than on clinical ideas that derive from classical libido theory. Nonetheless, Greenson feels it is important to evaluate a patient's predominant modes of experiencing inner tension and seeking pleasure in satisfying those tensions. He recognizes that libidinal organization and object relations are highly interdependent, but he finds the perspective of libido theory useful. This may in part be due to the fact that libido theory was a predominant psychoanalytic language when Greenson learned to be an analyst. Frequently, analysts trained many years apart will discuss clinical material using different theoretical models and languages, making it sound as if they disagree, when they are really in agreement.

[59] In his writings, Greenson (1967) says that "for mental health and above all for psychological-mindedness, primitive (mental) functions are needed to supplement the more highly differentiated ones" (p. 84). In the passage that follows this comes up where he talks about the patient's capacity to "play around with ideas." In order to be creative and get beyond the surface of psychological events to underlying, unconscious meanings, patients must have access to primary process thinking (condensation and displacement). In the initial interviews, it is important to assess for the ability to adaptively tap into these primitive mental functions in order to assess the patient's potential for insight.

*Greenson:* Yes, this is a factor to assess; *the length of time the patient has been struggling.* The *newness* of the illness. Now, what about assessing *libidinal organization?* I resent the fact that it sort of disappeared, it became old-fashioned. Gill doesn't even mention libidinal organization.[58] It's true, I don't think it's as important as the ego function assessment of the patient, but by God, if a man is functioning on some kind of an oral level, or an anal level, I think it matters. Again it is hard to assess in an initial interview, but you get some data that will help you to get a line on libidinal organization, particularly when it comes to a patient's relationship to objects: what quality of objects, what purpose, what instrumentality these objects mean to him. I don't think we should neglect the libidinal orientation. It makes a big difference if a man has the capacity to love and is jealous with his wife, than if a man has never been able to fall in love with anyone, and this relates to the libidinal organization.

*Candidate:* Along with the defense mechanisms, ego structure, weakness, and so on, it seems to me we have to evaluate in what points is he strong too. I guess we have mentioned this, but I don't want to only delve into the assessment of weaknesses, but also the evaluation of where there is strength in ego functioning.

*Greenson:* I agree, but that's part of what I subsumed under the heading of accomplishments and achievements. All right? But we not only evaluate the ego functions, we also try to get a line on strengths in the libidinal orientation of the patient as best we can.

## How Do You Appraise Psychological Mindedness?[59]

*Greenson:* Now, another main heading is: How to use the preliminary interviews to test the patient's psychological mindedness? We are all agreed that this is one of the most important factors in determining what we do with a patient.

[60] Here, Greenson is helping the candidates to consider the difference between open mindedness directed to the external world versus open mindedness applied to one's own internal world of thoughts, feelings, and fantasies. It is not surprising that he refers to segregation as an external issue, because this lecture was given in 1959, just before one of the most active periods of civil rights reform in the legislature in United States history.

So, what do you look for in determining a patient's psychological mindedness? It's not easy.

*Candidate:* It seems to me that psychological mindedness is made up of many, many different factors, some of which we have talked about. For instance, it seems to me that the rigidity of the individual has something to do with psychological mindedness. The plasticity of a person. Open mindedness.

*Greenson:* You mean things like: Is he against segregation?[60]

*Candidate:* I mean his ability to receive an idea and not immediately discard it, but to be open minded.

*Greenson:* I would agree that the ability to tolerate a fantasy, a supposition, a speculation, in terms of open mindedness, is essential. If you, in the course of talking, say, "I wonder if that's connected to what you said before," you need to see if he picks it up, can tolerate talking about connections. Does he play around with the ideas? Does he entertain the possibility, or does it mess him up too much that he doesn't know what you're talking about? If he rejects the idea it isn't so bad as it is if he just doesn't understand it. One of the important things that I try to do in all my preliminary interviews, is to make either some little interpretation, or some little connection or formulation. You know, I think, the fact of the baby drowning may have something to do with why you always get so upset when you go to the seashore. I want to see, what does she say to this. Does she not get it at all? Another way of doing this is to ask, "Do you have any notion about this, where does it come from?" You need to see how they react. Do they completely block on it or do they consider it?

*Candidate:* Even before you see his reaction to your intervention, you see how he organizes his own story, whether it's psychologically organized or whether it's on a basis of concrete facts.

*Greenson:* Very important point. How introspective has this man been about himself? Has he thought about himself? I don't mean his indulging in feeling sorry for himself, but a kind of contemplative introspectiveness. What does he tell you about himself, not only in terms of how much anxiety, how much depression, what symptoms, but in terms of his awareness of himself as a neurotic, or as a sufferer, as a person with troubles?

There are a few other things I have jotted down about psychological mindedness. One of them is: When this patient talks about other people, does he show any insight for them, does he show empathy for them? When you talk about your wife or you talk about your friends or colleagues, you are indicating your empathy or lack of empathy for them. So I think one of the things I like to listen for, and one of the things you see changing in analysis as patients get better, is their greater depth of understanding for others. Not only for themselves, for others. And sometimes they will reveal their psychological mindedness, their empathy, their capacity for empathy about others. For example, you get into a discussion of literature, or a play, or a movie, and you will often find this happening. You see how he describes a particular character, not that it has to be accurate or coincide with mine, that's not important, but the depth, the resonance, the dimension of the description.

*Naiveté, Honesty, and Psychological Mindedness*

*Candidate:* I have a general question. While I'm sure psychological mindedness is an important factor, there must be many patients who are naive psychologically, so how much can you rely on what you see in an initial interview?

*Candidate:* I think a person can be naive psychologically and still be psychologically minded.

*Greenson:* I agree, so when you get some evidence of a lack of psychological mindedness with a naive patient, you mustn't

[61] The point here is not to confuse a patient who has little knowledge of the psychological world (naive psychologically) with a patient who is incapable of doing the analytic work of seeking psychological insights (psychological mindedness). Conversely, it is important not to assume that the patient who can speak in psychological terms is psychologically minded. Anyone who has treated mental health professionals has probably experienced the way psychological savvy can become an intellectualized defense that compromises psychological mindedness.

[62] An important point made here is the need to search for psychological mindedness not only in terms of the direct capacity for self-observation, but in other areas as well. While Greenson does not explicitly say it here, the implication is that the discovery of psychological mindedness in any area of a patient's life (e.g., a writer's capacity to create characters that demonstrate the author's psychological mindedness), is a positive sign for the potential to be psychologically minded in the treatment.

[63] Greenson is suggesting here that psychopathology can consist of a person's capacity to tune into themselves and others. Here it seems Greenson is speaking of successful psychopaths, ones who get away with manipulating others for their own narcissistic purposes. There are, of course, also relatively unsuccessful psychopaths, whose manipulative efforts lead to recurrent punishments and even to jail. For these latter individuals, it seems the narcissism and superego pathology that accompanies psychopathology is not dependent on being very psychologically minded. Not all psychopaths are clever and shrewd.

jump to conclusions. You must try to find an area where you can find psychological mindedness in the relatively naïve person.[61]

*Candidate:* The opposite could be true of someone who has a great deal of psychological knowledge. I don't think it should be confused with psychological mindedness.

*Greenson:* Yes. So far we seem to be saying that patients who have psychological mindedness are better patients. I want to warn you that there is a pathological psychological mindedness. You see this in schizophrenics, who understand very well and can give you a brilliant insight and understanding about something going on in you or in them, but it's too much, too much. How come they see so much, why aren't the ordinary barriers present? You can see that. Pathological insight. You have to take the whole picture into account, because psychological mindedness can be problematic when it reaches beyond a certain quantity.

*Candidate:* I am wondering about some writers or artists whom I know, who obviously are very psychologically minded, but when you talk with them about themselves they turn it off. They create something insightful in their writing, but they don't see any of themselves in it, and they'll deny it when you talk with them about it.

*Greenson:* It can be very uneven.[62] People can be psychologically minded in certain areas, about certain things, about certain people, and extremely unpsychological in other areas. We want to see if it's there at all, and how much of it is there.

One other factor is the capacity for honesty as it is related to psychological mindedness. Some people will tell you what you're looking for instead of what they are feeling. The psychopath is psychologically minded, damned right he is, that's how he got to be a psychopath.[63] This is another aspect of pathological psychological mindedness, pathological in its use, as compared to the others which are pathological as to the extent. We didn't talk at all about looking for

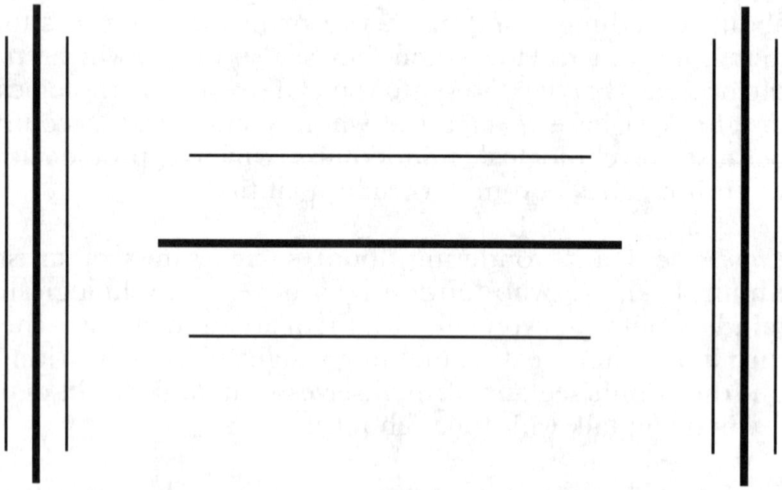

superego functions in the patient, and honesty would be one, along with the self-critical capacity.

I want to make one practical suggestion about psychological mindedness. One of the simplest ways of assessing it is when the patient will tell me something in the initial interview, face-to-face, and I look puzzled. I won't say anything. I'll just look puzzled and see if they pick it up. You know, whether they say, you seem puzzled, or whether they don't, if they just go on.

## How Empathy Relates to Psychological Mindedness

I think the main thing about psychological mindedness is the capacity for empathy. To be analyzed the patient needs empathy, you need it too to do the analysis, but goddamn it, they need it to understand the analysis. I have see many patients with a real block against being empathic due to some kind of hostilities or fears. Until they were analyzed they just couldn't understand my words. I think the nature of the therapeutic process is the mutual empathy, patient-therapist, therapist-patient.

*Candidate:* It may be somewhat premature in terms of later discussions, but are there techniques to facilitate a patient becoming psychologically minded?

Greenson: Analyzing the blocks to it. I feel everybody started out life being empathic and psychologically minded, or I think we'd all be schizophrenic, but most of us aren't empathic most of the time. I think the reason is we've lost it, it's been knocked out of us. It's been knocked out of us because it's a rather primitive way of communicating, and there are many more sophisticated ways that don't take as much energy, and that don't make you as vulnerable. To be intelligent, to use words, to exchange ideas, is much easier. Empathy involves letting yourself be touched by someone, and letting someone touch you. I think it was knocked out of us as we grew up.

[64] In this passage Greenson is referring to Spitz's observations of infants who were cared for physically but not emotionally, in that they were fed and changed, but they were not held or rocked. These infants slowly but surely lost interest in life, in some cases resulting in death. Blatt (1974) took these observations, applied them to adult depression, and delineated between anaclitic depression characterized by feelings of helplessness and emptiness, and introjective depression characterized by feelings of guilt, shame, and hopelessness.

Greenson takes the position that all humans are born with the capacity for empathy and psychological mindedness, but that these forms of human connections are developmentally primitive and vulnerable. He feels that as children grow up they get these capacities "knocked out of" them by the emotional challenges of childhood. As a result, he feels that empathy is not to be taught, but that the blocks to empathy can be removed by treatment, which will restore it. One point he clearly makes is that the therapist must have the capacity for empathy and psychological mindedness for the initial interviews to be successful.

[65] In 1960, a year after this lecture was given, Greenson wrote a paper called "Empathy and Its Vicissitudes." While it is uncertain if this is the specific paper he refers to here, it clearly shows his interest in the area of empathy and his commitment to the communication of psychoanalytic ideas. When he says below that he would like to give the paper at the "International" he refers to the International Psychoanalytic Association, which has scientific meetings at different locations around the world every two years. Here Greenson is saying that understanding empathy is a subject of international importance.

*Candidate:* You see it in children.

*Greenson:* I think all mother–child relationships were essentially empathic, basically nonverbal. The mother feels for the baby, the baby feels for the mother. They respond to each other nonverbally, and I think that's why babies live. If they don't have it, they develop apathy and they die. It's the anaclitic depression of Spitz.[64] Most of the time you can analyze the blocks to empathy, but sometimes it's very hard. It is only possible to analyze the blocks to empathy, it can't be taught. I see it in my patients, as they get better through analysis they seem to develop more empathy. I have patients who develop the capacity to feel my moods, but it's very subjective and unreliable.

*Candidate:* You can also see empathy develop in a patient's relationship to others.

*Greenson:* Yes. They pick up clues and clues that ordinarily they didn't notice. They are more responsive. Not that they react more necessarily, but they are more aware of other people's feelings and particular nuances that they didn't see. They see new depths they never saw, and a lot of this is the increase in the capacity for empathy. I once started a paper on this and I have worked a little more on that paper.[65] I'd like to give it at the International because I think it's an extremely important subject. It's the whole essence of psychological mindedness, and the whole business of the initial interview is very much hinged on the capacity to empathize with little information. It's so hard to empathize with someone that you hardly know. You ask, what occurs to you about this? Do you have any notion about so-and-so, any idea about where this comes from? Just to see, can they get off the ground.

**What Is the Role of the Patient's History?**

What about historical material? Sure you get a preliminary interview, you appraise the patient in variety of ways, and

[66] This is a reference to Merton Gill, who emphasized the importance of transference over all other sources of information, and who questioned the idea of factual, historical information uninfluenced by transference. It is interesting to note that here Greenson refers to the history as "factual information," given the current controversies over memories being objective and factual versus subjective and narrative. Greenson clearly was of the opinion that there is factual history that can provide some objective data about the patient.

[67] Greenson describes taking two to three hours for the initial interviews, and one to two sessions for the transition to the couch. This is probably not much different from current-day practice where analytic patients are concerned, but it is much longer than for the typical managed care patients, where in the extreme only a total of five to six sessions will be reimbursed for the entire assessment and treatment.

It is instructive to compare Greenson's methods for his private practice of psychoanalysis, with the methods he described in the section "Historical Remarks" (p. 19–21) on his work with the draft board in 1941, assessing men's capacity to serve in the Army. In the Army the initial interviews were only one to two minutes long, but it's clear that only a few key issues were being determined as a basis for a general psychiatric screening decision. In this section, he weighs the desire to have information, the disruption of having to stop the patient frequently during the treatment to ask for information, against the desire to get the treatment going and not have a protracted period of initial interviews. Clearly there is no ideal solution, but a challenge to find the best fit between competing requirements of the preliminary interviews and the treatment itself.

it's a relatively unstructured situation, but what about historical data? Isn't there an importance or a value to historical material? Do you want it or do you completely ignore it? What's the answer? Do you want present information, history, or both?

My impression is the following: For the first part of the preliminary interview, I let the patient take me where he wants. I do very little guiding into anything. But toward the end of the first hour, although I usually take more than an hour, but before I'm through, I want to get some historical data. I know Gill[66] and his cohorts go way out against factual material, but I think they go overboard. Before I'm through with the preliminary interviews, I want to get some picture of this man's history; both his present situation and his early history. It's not just habit. I think there's something of a benefit in hearing the story of the continuity of a person's life, and not just fragments. A person's life is not just a series of fragments, fitted together, there's a certain continuity to it, and I would like to get a picture of that continuity.

When I am through with the preliminary interviews, I like my patients to have a present, a past, and a future. Now I don't know their future, but I like to sketch it. It's the future that makes me determine whether I'm going to take him or not, and part of the future comes from his past and what he's done with his past in terms of his present. I say, I would like a picture of you, tell me about you; as general as this. But then I will say, after a while, if I have the time before I'm through, what about your childhood? Again I want to see what he says. Does he talk about his mother, his father, what he was like as a kid?

## When Do You Get a Detailed History?[67]

*Candidate:* What about a situation where the patient is appraised and is going into analysis with you. You have decided he would be a good patient, but when the patient is still sitting up you would say, I'd like to know as much about

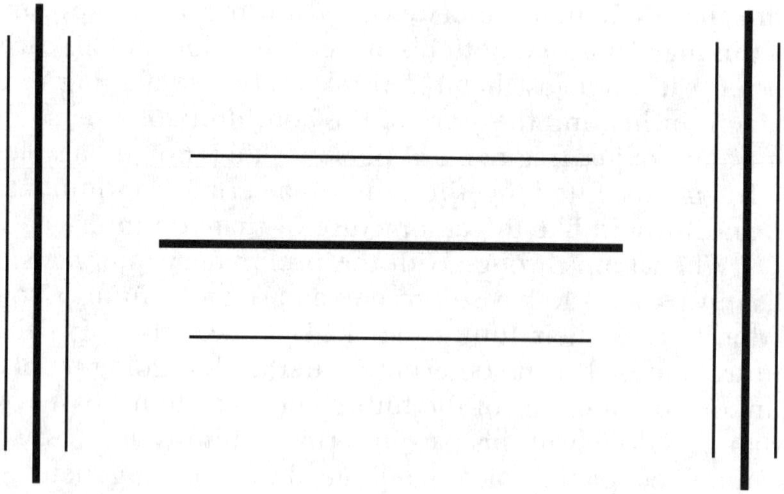

you as you can tell me. This is not part of the appraisal, but afterwards.

*Greenson:* I agree with this. I do this all the time when I have decided I am going to analyze the patient and the patient agrees to be analyzed. Before I say, now we'll do free association, I want to fill out the outline of my picture of him, but there I want to be careful. I don't want him to tell me all he knows about himself because that may take too long. I want a kind of framework, so I won't have to stop him every two minutes, and say, this nursemaid, when was this? Or when did you live in Connecticut? I'd like a certain outline of periods in his life, a kind of sketch of his development. I do ask my patients before I put them on the couch: Now before we go to the analytic work, I'd like a picture, a kind of an outline of your life. I often say: It is so I don't have to stop you and interrupt you and ask who is this and when was that.

*Candidate:* Getting this sketch of the patient sounds like it may take two interviews.

*Greenson:* I would say it usually takes at least one or two interviews, in addition to the two or three interviews that it's taken for the preliminary interviews. By and large I take about two or three hours for preliminary interviews, and about one or two additional hours to make the transition to the couch, which includes getting the sketch of the patient's life, but here we are getting ahead of ourselves. Enough for today.

## March 4, 1959: Preliminary Interviews—Lecture III

*Greenson:* So far we have covered the ego functions of the patient, the psychological mindedness of the patient, and now the next major heading is the patient's motivation. All of this has to do with what you look for and what you try to accomplish during the preliminary interviews. Under ego functions we included: (1) Is the patient in contact and how

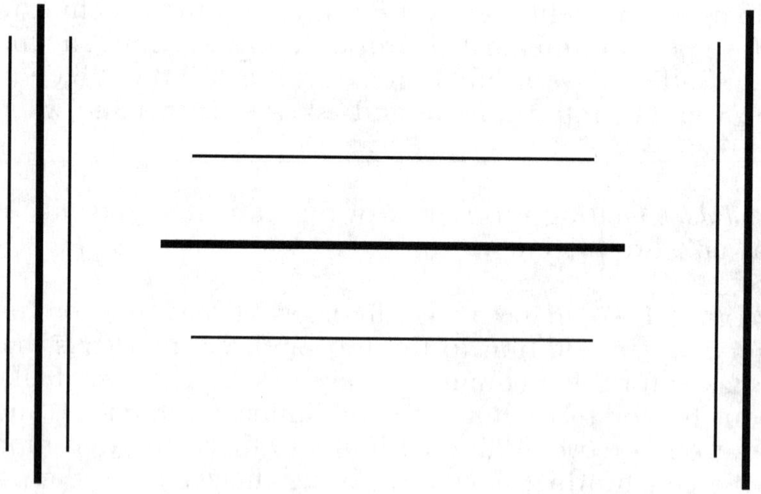

is the patient in contact? (2) What kind of object relation-ships does this patient seem capable of establishing and maintaining? (3) What are the patient's affects like, are they appropriate affects, are they bizarre affects? (4) What is the instinct–defense balance, is there impulsivity, equilibrium? (5) The accomplishments of the patient. The interests of the patient. (6) Intelligence. Thinking capacity. (7) The kind of anxiety and depressiveness. (8) The kinds of de-fenses. Here I also have the symptoms, because they tell you something about the patient's ego functions. (9) Reality testing. Is this patient influenceable? The rigidities of the patient. (10) How much of the personality is invaded by the illness? In fact, a lot of these don't really belong under ego functions of the patient, but they are the kinds of things I think about, and that I think we discussed.

## Appraising the Motivation of the Patient

*Is the Motivation Internal or External?*

Let's go on today to discussing the motivation of the patient. What do you look for in terms of the patient's motivations? I think the first major differentiation in terms of motivation has to do with this: Is this patient essentially internally moti-vated or externally motivated? In other words, is this person coming for help for inner reasons, pain, misery, depression, anxiety, whatever, or is it essentially because someone is pushing him or her in some form or other. I think this is the first major differentiation that you have to make.

Let me give you an example of what I mean. I get a call from and make an appointment to see a woman who is obviously distressed, suffering, sad, and depressed. The story

[68] The difference between internal and external motivation is not always so clear, as Greenson points out here. If a patient goes into treatment and works to change primarily in order to secure some external goal (e.g., to save a marriage), Greenson considers this more external motivation, even though the patient may be willing to work to change. Why? Because the patient may drop the treatment as soon as the marriage seems okay, even though the internal issues have not changed at all. Greenson thinks in terms of internal motivation where the inner issues are the goal, not just a means to another goal. This point of view is a hallmark of psychoanalysis, and clearly differs from treatments that aim to bring about symptomatic relief efficiently.

is, her husband left her. They are married 22 years. She thought it was a good marriage and she wakes up one morning and gets a letter from him which is a "Dear Mary" letter—the counterpart of the "Dear John" letter—saying, I haven't been happy for many years, I'm moving out, and I think you ought to see a psychiatrist.

Now I see this woman who has been married 22 years and her husband suddenly leaves her and she comes in very miserable and upset, but the fact that she's miserable and upset isn't enough. The point is, what is she upset about? I quickly see she comes to see me because she's miserable over losing her husband, but more than that, I see that she comes to see me because in the back of her mind the notion is: If I will go to see you, and if I will listen to you, and if I will undergo treatment, if I will change, my husband will come back. Now essentially this is an externally determined motivation. She is coming to see me in order to get her husband to come back.[68]

Now this is different from another kind of a patient, and I'll take a woman again, who gets a note or a phone call or something from her husband saying that he has left her. Again like with the first case, after many years of marriage this woman is shocked. Then they talk and he says: "I have been miserable these many years." She answers him by saying, "My God why have you been miserable?" At first he doesn't answer her but confronts her and says, "Well, don't you know why? Think a moment. Why? Because every time I would want to bring someone home for dinner, you said, oh, so much work; and every time I said, let's go on a vacation, you said we can't afford it; and every time I wanted intercourse you said, oh my God, I'm tired; and all of our life was working, making money. It's been all kinds of things that have nothing to do with pleasure, nothing to do with fun, nothing to do with joy. This is a grind which we were both in, where we just had to protect ourselves from terrible dangers and from poverty or from unhappiness or difficulty. That's why I don't want to live with you." Now the wife was horror stricken by this, and she said, "Please, I'll change, I'll do anything you want." And the husband said, "I don't

believe you. I think you'd like to do anything I want, but you can't. You're kidding yourself. You can't. This is the way you are. I just realized it now, but I've been a fool begging you to stay with me when we had these quarrels. I don't want any more."

Now this woman whom I'm talking about comes to see me and says very weepingly: "He's right, he's right. I never realized it so clearly, but it's true. I didn't want sex." And then this woman whom I'm describing would say, "It's a funny thing, you know, I really wanted the sex, but he would approach me and my first reaction was no. Then I'd think about it for a while, and I'd realize that I would like to have sex, but I'd be proud or stubborn or something like that and I wouldn't ask him. Or he'd come over and give me a kiss and I'd push him away and say: Listen, I have to do the dishes, but then I'd think, oh, I don't have to do dishes right now, but something would keep me from going over and putting my arm around him. Or he would say, well, let's go to Palm Springs and my first reaction would be no, and then I'd think, oh, we could go, but I'd think, better to save the money. I don't know why I had to be that way, but that's the way I was." At this point I asked her what made her aware of this? She said, "When he told me after all the years that we've been married, and all the times I threatened to divorce him and he'd come begging, when this time he didn't come begging but he said he's through with me, and I could see he meant it, I suddenly realized there is something wrong with me."

So I then talk with this particular woman—and now I'm trying to contrast the two women—and I said, oh, what you'd like is to get your husband back, and she said, "Yes, I would, but I think there's more that's wrong with me. I think if he came back I would do the same things again." So I said, well you must have some idea why you do this. She said, "I figure, my mother and father fought all my life long. I ran away from home when I was 16. All I ever saw at home was my mother and father fighting." To which I said, so without your being able to control it, this is what you did too. Your husband said yes, and you said no. Your husband

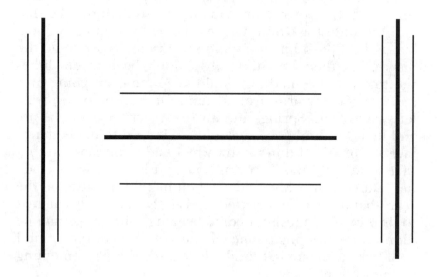

said no, you said yes, at which point she agreed that maybe I was right. What I'd like you to see is that this woman also wanted her husband back, but in addition to wanting her husband back, she is disconnected with herself, she doesn't like what she is. She doesn't like how she is. In addition to the external forces pushing her there's an internal force pushing her to change. This is another kind of motivation.

### How Much Pain Is Involved?

Second is, how much pain is involved? Is it a trivial pain, or is it a real important, severe pain? Is it a major area of satisfaction, of enjoyment, of accomplishment that's being interfered with, or is it a minor one? The patient comes and complains that, "You know, I have a tremor, and when I'm having tea, it embarrasses me, or when I'm dealing the cards, it embarrasses me." Now I submit to you that this doesn't interest you one whit, whether she trembles having the tea or dealing the goddam cards, unless she gives this as an example, and she then tells you about other situations when she is being watched, that she trembles not only in her hands, but inwardly, and she feels terribly self-conscious. This particular patient I'm talking about couldn't walk into a room of people without this terrible trembling. Her voice would crack and tremble when she walked into a room. When she went to her daughter's class to talk to the teacher she would be embarrassed and blush and flush. This woman was an actress, and very comfortable on the stage because it wasn't herself, she was playing a role and she was some-body else. But in her own house, or at a party where people knew who she was, then she had this terrible self-conscious-ness. So, the pain has to be considerable and has to interfere with some major satisfaction or accomplishment.

### Is the Patient Curious about the Pain?

Now I think another aspect of the testing out of the patient's motivation has to do with: Does this patient want to under-stand her pain? In other words, I'm always impressed by

patients who not only want to get rid of the pain but have a curiosity about what is it? Why am I this way? How come? In addition to the wish to get rid of the pain, it's a curiosity. What makes me tick. This kind of curiosity is a very valuable addition to the motive of getting rid of pain. Often when you start to do analysis with a patient, unless there is also this additional motivation, the curiosity, they get rid of the symptom and experience a flight into health. I think the curiosity is another aspect of the psychological mindedness, so you see these things overlap.

### External Factors That Influence Motivation

Now part of the testing of the motivation has to do also I think with the external obstacles. Up until now we were talking about the motivation, the positive drive to get well. I think we ought to add, not only external factors which make a patient want to get treatment, or push them into treatment, but also external factors that interfere with motivation. For example, money. In people who are financially very hard pressed, the fact that analysis takes a considerable amount of money can be a minus motivation, and may be one of the reasons they would say, well, I'm not sure. Or time, the time. Or travel time, distance. I recently saw a woman in consultation who is the wife of a psychiatrist. The more she talked the more I heard her saying: Is it worth dragging five times a week and paying $100 a week for treatment, after all, how much is an orgasm worth? And my God, now the kids are finally big enough to go to grammar school, and they're out of the house. And I have some free time and leisure. And I'm going to give this up dragging here? Maybe it's better to have the kids at home than to drag here. I heard this all the time we were talking, so I confronted her with it by asking her, is it worth it? And she said, "Not to me, not to me." I then said, is it worth it to your husband? She said, "Yes, to my husband it's worth it, he says it's worth it." So, the external obstacles which interfere with motivation have to be taken into account.

[69] The section addresses the fact that patients can come for treatment with the acute onset of symptoms, and if the trigger for the distress is an external problem that improves, the symptoms improve, and the motivation for treatment is gone. With chronic conditions, the symptoms may not go away, but the patient has learned to live with them. Greenson goes into these issues because he does not want to begin an analysis if the patient is likely to end it prematurely, or if the patient will lack the motivation needed for analytic progress. This is obviously a very different situation where symptomatic relief is the goal and the treatment is psychotherapy.

## Secondary Gain and Motivation

Finally, the secondary gain from the neurosis has to be considered in assessing motivation. People who have neurotic problems very often have developed a life in which they gain some kind of advantage from the neurosis, and they come to you for treatment because they have pain or because other people push them or a combination of both internal and external factors. The question still is, is it worth it? Take an agoraphobic who has had agoraphobia for twenty-five years, and the husband has geared his life such that he never lets his wife go alone anywhere, he is always there to accompany her. The children know mother must never be alone, they have to report to mother, and friends know that this is a special case, she can never do anything unless you can accompany her. The whole world has been arranged around taking special consideration and care and interest that she is excluded from certain difficulties or nuisances. When you talk about treatment with this woman, you will be amazed at how many places you will bump into the fact that she will have to give up certain special satisfactions and considerations. If she went to a movie everyone let her have the aisle seat, because she also had a touch of claustrophobia. When she went to a concert others always got the tickets for her, and at parties people never asked her why she disappeared early, because it was her phobia. Sometimes one would envy her, like if it was a dull party and she would get to disappear, and you'd think: Brother!

## Acute Onset of Symptoms versus Chronic Conditions[69]

I think we ought to add here that the more recent the onset of symptoms, the more acute the onset of symptoms, the more likely the motivation will be stronger. The longer the symptoms have been endured and the slower they came on, the less urgent will be the need for help and treatment. People who have learned to live with their illness have less motivation than people who haven't yet had to live with it.

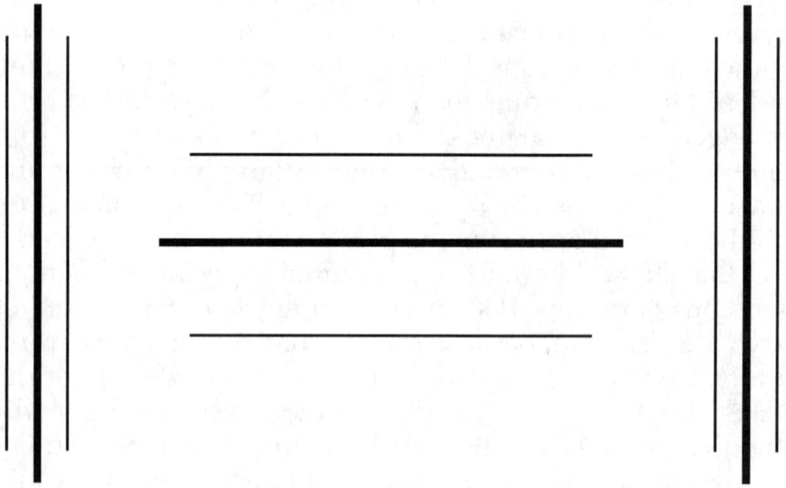

Now I wonder what you have to add about different aspects of the patient's motivation?

*Candidate:* What about character neurosis and patients who say, I want very much to free myself, something is missing from my life.

*Greenson:* I certainly have seen these kind of patients, but what kind of special problem of motivation is this? How is this different from someone who says, I don't get as much sexual satisfaction as I would like? What is the difference in motivation?

*Candidate:* The patient with the character neurosis doesn't want to get rid of any specific symptoms.

*Greenson:* Oh, but the fact that they're not getting enough out of life, the fact that life is empty, is something ego alien. It's more subtle and harder to pin down than a symptom, but I'm rather impressed with how many patients I have seen with just this complaint. But what about problems of motivation when you start seeing a patient?

*Candidate:* Sometimes it's difficult at the beginning to know how much the patient is suffering, what the patient really wants, or how much of it will last. I have a young woman who came with the best of motivation, very naive about analysis, but we discussed the five times a week, etc., and everything was fine. Now, a few months later, when the symptoms have decreased and the long haul begins, there is a reevaluation of the motivation. You wonder if this change of motivation could have been evaluated during the acute symptomatology.

*Greenson:* Well, I think acute situational disturbances which are precipitated by acute situational problems, let's say an unhappy love affair, are always suspect in this way. The patient comes out of being rejected by a sweetheart, or the death of a sweetheart, something like this, and agrees she or he needs treatment. They realize they have all kinds of

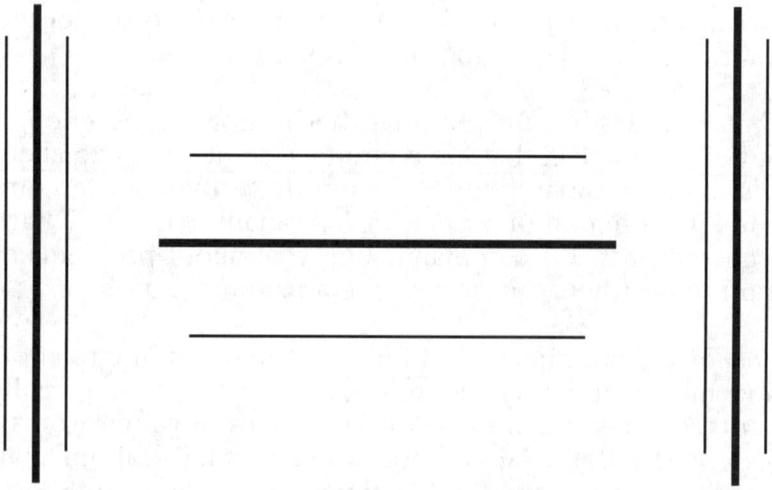

troubles, and you make all the arrangements. Then the external situation changes. Either another man comes along, or they fall in love, or they meet somebody new, or their old one comes back, or even quick insights make a real change and a loss of the symptoms. At this point, you see that the real deeper motivation isn't there, or it is obscured. It certainly happens.

*Factors That Change Motivation During Treatment*

*Candidate:* Well, this was a little different, because it was a postpartum depression, and we got to the stage where the depression lifted. Then you have to understand it in relation to the transference and what goes on in the analysis, but a problem of motivation came about due to the development of a positive transference.

*Greenson:* That's an interesting point that you're bringing up. In addition to the problem of motivation in the beginning when you assess the patient, there is the problem of a change in motivation that happens when, for example, the patient develops an acute sexual transference. Now instead of coming for treatment because they want to get rid of symptoms or neurosis, they come out of love for you. Now the reasons a patient is coming is neurosis, schmeurosis, it's "Doctor, I love you, and if you want me to come I'll come, but the hell with this Freud stuff, let's go to the couch," and they don't mean for free association. God knows, this happens almost routinely with women patients, though it also happens with the men.

*Candidate:* Or the opposite happens and they react with anxiety and run.

*Greenson:* I see patients running from the positive transference far less often. I more often see this whole shift in motivation in the transference. It becomes, for love of you I will do the analysis. I can think or fantasize in some way I might

[70] Here Greenson seems to be saying that there is something important missing from this candidate's clinical description, such that it does not portray a real person. His comment demonstrates how he is not just listening for signs and symptoms, but he is trying to get a feel for the whole person.

In this case, the candidate's patient comes for help with a postpartum depression, which lifts after several months, and is followed by a positive feeling about life and the analyst. After about four to five months the depression returns but the candidate says it's all in the transference, yet it's not clear what this looks like during the sessions. Greenson comments about the fact that he cannot get a feeling for this person. Perhaps it is because there is not enough detail.

In any event, given that this is a section about motivation, it is noteworthy that there is no sense in the candidate's clinical description of what would cause the return of a depression restricted to the transference. Without some sense of the motivation, Greenson cannot get a grasp on the patient as a real person, all he has is a symptom (which could mean a dozen different things in a dozen different people). His confusion is also interesting given his emphasis on forming a relationship with the patient, and the fact that there is no sense of this candidate's relationship with the patient.

get you, or I might influence you. This positive sexual transference can become an obstacle in the working analysis, but
usually they quit analysis when the analyst does not handle
the transference well, when he shows fear of the transference because of countertransference reactions against it.
Then I have seen the patient run from the analysis because
of the fear of positive sexual transference.

*Candidate:* Well, it's not only the thought of the sexual transference, it's also the finding of the mother as the depression
lifts. First, the depression lifts because of the relationship
with you. Then you become the good maternal object for a
time, which eventually begins to break down, bringing the
patient face-to-face with some of the depression that it still
there. It has been uncovered by finding such a wonderful,
understanding person, then it returns in the positive transference.

*Greenson:* I can imagine this and I think I know what you
mean.

*Candidate:* After four or five months of analysis, the depression is gone, and everything is fine. I'm wonderful and she's
wonderful and everybody is wonderful, except the depression begins to develop again, and it's all in the transference.
Except she says she feels fine now so why face this, why not
just leave? She says she loves her baby, she loves her husband, and I'm a great fellow, but why go on with all this just
to find out what's going on.

*Greenson:* I must say that the picture you draw just doesn't
come to life, but maybe it's just that I can't follow you.[70] At
any rate, it just doesn't seem alive to me. You probably have
a patient in mind, but you don't want to get involved in
telling about it. I think of a depressive patient I have treated
for God knows how many years in psychotherapy, a woman.
And it's true when she is miserable and depressed she comes
for her treatment, and when she starts to feel better, she
doesn't come. I must say it doesn't break my heart, although
I think of her with anxiety from time to time. It's been two

months since I've seen her now, and I know something will happen. It will be an anniversary of the death of her son, or someone will mention the death of a child, or she will read about death in the paper, or one of her grandchildren will get a cold or be sick, then she'll come. And when things start to get better she just doesn't show up. One sees such things.

Let's get back to assessing motivation in the preliminary interviews, prior to psychoanalytic treatment. The changes in motivation that happen during the course of treatment are different kinds of problems. I'm talking about assessing the patient and coming to a conclusion about what kind of therapy the patient needs. One of the factors that I think is of major importance is the motivation.

## Reinforcing Motivation During the Initial Interviews

I think incidentally that because of the importance of the factor of motivation, during these interviews you should try to constantly reinforce the motivation. For example, when a patient comes and tells me about her husband leaving her, then she tells me she was a killjoy and a wet blanket, she didn't want sex, she didn't want to go on vacations, I say to her, my God, what a miserable way of living. You haven't ever lived. In other words, I not only agree with her, I add to it. Or a patient has a phobia, and tells me that the phobia is interfering with this and that. As I see other things I add to it, and say, well, you see, it's not only interfered with this and that, but it's also interfered with your enjoyment of your children. Look at this, what self-esteem do you have, so you did write this book, great, you're afraid to do so and so.

In other words, I constantly add to the motivation in the initial interviews. I don't only do it in the initial interviews, I do it forever after, whenever an opportunity presents itself which I think is appropriate I will say, look how your symptoms interfere. I went to underline this point because this goes from the first interview till years later. I like to show

[71] The process of "freshening the motivation" by pointing out the patient's problems gets to a crucial difference between psychoanalytic treatments and treatments that target symptom relief. In the managed care model, for example, one would not seek to increase a patient's discomfort to increase their desire for treatment. In fact, the opposite is true. All efforts are made to bring relief of discomfort so the treatment can be completed as soon as possible. By comparison, psychoanaytic treatments in general and psychoanalysis in particular aim to help a patient see where their capacity for living a fuller life could be greater, and then to expand that capacity. The patient's mental health is seen in a much broader context than just current symptoms that are disturbing. It is important to keep in mind that patients enter into psychoanalytic treatment knowing that the primary goal is not symptom relief, and that they have given consent. All treatments have upsides and downsides, including medications, where patients must be willing to tolerate unwanted side effects in order to get the desired benefits.

[72] Although Greenson takes up neurotic motives in this section, and he includes neurotic motives in both the patient and the analyst, there are reality needs that can be problematic sources of motivation as well. For example, there are patients who have no friends other than their therapist, and the same can be true of the therapist, or the therapist can need the patient for financial or other reasons.

the patient where the symptoms have interfered with his way of living, his way of enjoyment, his way of accomplishment. I don't like to leave it until the patient is ready to quit to point out where the symptoms interfere, but I don't do it at times when it will make the patient unduly depressed or anxious. But I recognize that a certain amount of motivation must be present to keep a patient in analysis, otherwise why the hell should they do it. Analysis is the most painful, costly, time consuming, awkward kind of treatment. We are analysts and we take for granted that analysis is a rational and even quite exhilarating experience, but for the ordinary patient, it is a swift pain. I would say that as much as I want the initial interviews to be of therapeutic benefit, I want to reinforce the motivation of the patient, given that I feel there is a probability that the patient is willing and able to go on and do some therapy. In fact, I reinforce and freshen the motivation throughout the analysis.[71]

*Candidate:* There must be certain situations where you wouldn't.

*Greenson:* When treatment is impossible or difficult, or when other considerations are more important. When the patient, let's say, is on the verge of going into a severe depression, and by herself says, "Look how I've screwed up my life, look what waste of my time, look what I have done with my husband, look what I have done with my children." This is no time for me to say oh yes, and your grandchildren have suffered as well. This is no time to reinforce motivation. But I do think you need a considerable amount of motivation to go on in analysis. If you're not interested in becoming an analyst, you probably just want to be a neurotic and finish treatment.

*Neurotic Motives in the Patient and the Analyst*[72]

*Candidate:* What about situations where a prospective patient comes to the analyst with certain expectation and a

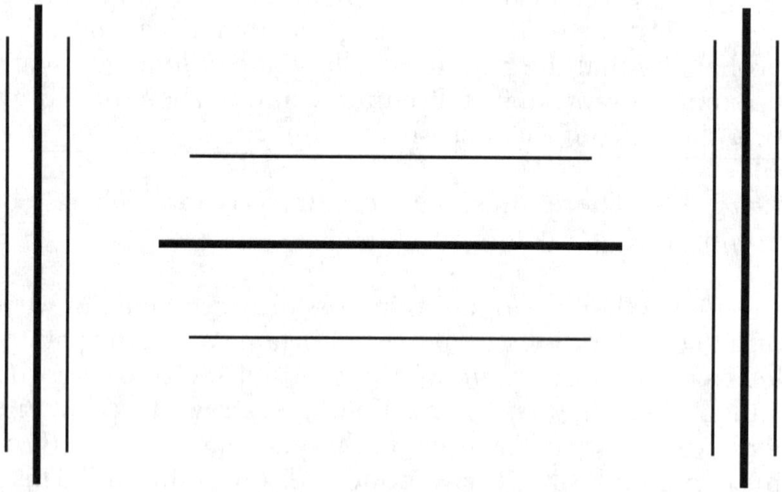

ready-made transference that involves a neurotic choice of the analyst. Maybe choosing the best analyst in town to show that even the best analyst in town can't cope with them. Let's say, it's a kind of play analysis that is more sparring with the analyst than anything else.

*Greenson:* You're bringing up an interesting point here. This has to do with complications of the motivation, sort of secondary or auxiliary motivations. Often these kinds of people are somewhat paranoid, this kind of person who is going to try to do something to the analyst. I've seen one man like that who wanted to go into analysis because his wife went into analysis. He was envious that she was going to get something that he wasn't going to get, and this was the only motivation. He turned out to be quite paranoid. I've heard other instances where people want analysis because they want to get even with their father or something. When this is the main kind of motivation they are apt to be kind of paranoid.

*Candidate:* Isn't this what we should evaluate during the initial interview, and not recommend an analysis for a person like this, even though we may see a neurosis?

*Greenson:* These are neurotic motivations you're talking about, in which the person seeks treatment because they are in a competitive position to someone else who is in treatment. I think you are talking about the problem of prestige that goes along for certain people in being analyzed, particularly by certain prominent analysts. God knows, I have seen this. I have been really pestered by certain people, who have written letters to me or called me on the phone many times because they know me as a prominent speaker, or as a professor at the medical school, or as now dean of the training school. They want to go to me in particular, not just for the prestige of being in treatment with me, but with the desire to defeat me. But let's discuss this when we discuss the choice of analysts, or the problems in selecting the analyst. We'll talk about this after we have decided a person should

be analyzed, and on the basis of what we have done, we are deciding who to send them to. Then I would like to talk about such persons.

But I do believe there are patients who seek you out and who have a special motivation to come to you for certain obscure reasons. I don't ever take a patient when the motivation is obscure. I make it a point to make it easy for people with poor motivation or obscure motivation to run away quickly. Rather than be helpful and eager to get them into treatment, I'm uneager, very uneager. If I think they're going to run because I won't see them right away, I'll say: I'm sorry, I don't have time to see you this next couple of days, so we will have to wait a week. I will bring up with such patients painful realities about the treatment, to increase their running away from the analysis. But in patients where I suspect that the motivation is substantial, I will do all kinds of things to deepen the motivation. When I suspect it isn't very substantial, I do all kinds of things to help them run.

*Candidate:* I think this is a very dangerous thing to do.

*Greenson:* Why?

*Candidate:* I think they say they're coming for this reason, and yet one has to be very careful that you haven't missed the real reason. If you make too early a judgment, you may help them out of treatment where perhaps they could have been helped by treatment.

*Greenson:* I'm always careful, but I'm also careful not to waste my time, or anybody else's time. It's precious. Let's take the examples of the two women I gave you before, both of whom had husbands who left them, one of whom I sensed had some real, deep motivation for treatment, and the other I suspected only wanted to get her husband back. The one who I sensed only wanted her husband back later told me why she came to me. It was because her husband had said to her once, "Most analysts are a bunch of hot air, the only

one I think is any good is Greenson." She came to me to please her husband. I felt she would quit instantly if he came back, or it would drag on for God knows how long until he came back. But I also felt that if she were to hear that her husband had decided to get a divorce and to marry someone else she would quit treatment.

When we began to talk about why she needed help, I began in my ordinary way to try to point up things that would increase her motivation. I very slowly became aware that this wasn't very deep motivation, because I found her constantly defending herself. For example, in the beginning she was saying, "Oh yes, I wasn't very good to him," slowly I found that in the last half of the first interview already she was saying, "But my God, as recently as six weeks ago, we had a wonderful time sexually." Mind you he has left her in part because sexually she was never terribly interested and now she tells me this. Whereas before she was ready to admit that she needed help because he had said, go get help. Now she was starting to defend herself. She started to tell me about how he would accuse her of being the dominant one in the family, but he left all the decisions up to her, and she was just trying to be helpful.

Now I began to hear more and more of her defenses, more and more of her rationalizations, and I slowly got the idea that rather than increase her motivation, what would happen if I started to agree with her? I ended the first interview rather inconclusively and said, look, we have to talk some more. The next time she was still pretty miserable, but I now began to tell her that although her husband says she needs treatment, I'm not convinced, I really am not convinced. I asked her to talk about why she felt she needed treatment, which was a very different tack than I had taken earlier. She started to tell me how when they first had intercourse she was the one who initiated it, because he was too afraid. I found her trying to persuade me that the husband who left her was the severely neurotic man. I let her go on and on and toward the end of the time I said, I think I'm convinced your husband really had some problems, and I can see that he was unhappy with you, but what's this got

[73] In this section a candidate has expressed concern that Greenson is not doing enough to encourage motivation in the patient. A worry that a patient who needs treatment might decide against it without more encouragement. The candidate even says what Greenson is doing may be "dangerous." In fact, Greenson is not pushing patients out of treatment, nor is he discouraging them. In a number of ways he is allowing their doubts to be raised and considered seriously. In this way, he makes sure that any decision to pursue treatment comes from the patient's motivation not his motivation.

Greenson does not wish to "sell" his patients on treatment, though he is willing to help them appreciate how much they are suffering, even in ways they have not considered, and what analytic treatment might offer them. If he gets the feeling that a patient wants to cover over his suffering despite Greenson's attempts to highlight the problems, however, he will give the patient the room to decline treatment, or to seek some other form of help that is a better fit with their level of motivation.

to do with your treatment? Again I left it rather inconclusive, but now I was no longer trying to increase her motivation. Quite the contrary, I was sort of making her prove to me she needed treatment. I told her we needed to take a little more time and asked her to come one more time.

She came a third time and said: "In all honesty, I don't think I need treatment. I certainly don't think I need analysis.[73] I only find few of my friends are sympathetic with me. I have the feeling they really sympathize with my husband. You know, I really have no one to talk to." I said, if you need somebody to talk to, let's make arrangements for you to have someone who will talk to you. So by the end of the third interview I had more or less concluded with her that what she needed was someone to talk to, not analysis. She was nowhere near ready for analysis, but she needed to see a psychotherapist with experience, because these are very tough cases. She needed to see an experienced analyst who wanted a psychotherapy case, or someone who has lived a lot and who will really know how to handle this. I sent her to an analyst who saw her occasionally and did a very nice job.

Handling motivation is crucial, considering the fact that in the last thirteen years I've only had one patient who didn't want to come back to see me. That was a case an out-of-town analyst pestered me about, saying over and over that this was a very important case because this man was a big wheel, this man's wife was a bigger wheel, this man's daughter was the biggest wheel, and this family had millions of dollars. He said, "Romi, please see these people!" Finally, I said, all right, I'll see them, but I must say I really botched it up. It was awkward because I was resentful about having this analyst pester me. The girl didn't like me, and I must say I didn't like her either. It was just not natural. I was annoyed with that idiot analyst and the way he brought the case to me, so the girl never came back.

*Candidate:* What about cases where I'm interested and my curiosity is aroused? My curiosity about the patient could provide enough of a lever to get them into analysis. It also seems conceivable that some countertransference issues within myself may make some patients appear less motivated than they really are.

[74] This comment about the "other group" refers to the other psychoanalytic institute in the Los Angeles area affiliated with the American Psychoanalytic Association. Greenson was a member of the Los Angeles Psychoanalytic Institute and Society, as opposed to the "other group," the Southern California Psychoanalytic Institute.

[75] Even though Greenson is talking about neurotic needs here, this section can also include consideration of the therapist's real needs. Greenson clearly had a very successful practice during the heyday of psychoanalysis. Nowadays, due to managed care, therapists are finding their fees reduced without their control, and the number of sessions permitted is often dramatically reduced as well. If patients have managed care benefits and a therapist accepts them, the patient may not be permitted to pay for more therapy privately, even if he or she wishes to do so. The overall impact of this revolution in the health care insurance industry has been to make it more difficult for patients to get access to certain types of psychotherapy, and more difficult for psychotherapists and psychoanalysts to maintain their income levels. As a result, therapists may need their patients more than ever from a financial standpoint.

This financial situation has to be openly appreciated by therapists or the need for the patient can cloud the therapist's judgment. In a manner similar to what Greenson is discussing here, Sidney Smith, a very talented psychoanalyst and psychologist, used to say (when he taught classes in analytic treatment approaches) that it is "difficult to do good analytic work until the therapist has a waiting list of patients." In other words, it is difficult to do good analytic work until the therapist has no need for a given patient to fill hours. The penetrating honesty required to look at such issues openly and directly is essential for transference based approaches to treatment. For example, is the therapist afraid to confront issues that might anger the patient for fear that the patient will drop out of treatment and it will mean a loss of income that cannot be easily replaced?

*Greenson:* That's certainly true. The analyst's motivation can obscure or uncover the patient's motivations for better or worse. On Saturday I saw a man who told me he had a consultation with an analyst of many years' experience, an analyst in the other group incidentally.[74] He and his wife had consulted this analyst because of a marital problem. The analyst listened to both of them and said, "I find you are both healthy people who are incompatible, so I cannot object to the fact that you want a divorce." Well, I was really shocked by this and I even doubted that it was true. I listened to this man tell the story of a very unhappy marriage, in which quite early he gave in to his wife's sexual peculiarities, but I couldn't for the life of me see the other analyst's decision, because both seemed severely neurotic. That they were incompatible is also true, but they were neurotics. Then I had an appointment with her alone and then with him alone, but I didn't see how a divorce would solve anything. They both needed some therapy. I wasn't sure how much therapy they both needed.

Anyway, I called up the analyst and I said to him, I saw these people and I was sort of puzzled by your recommendations. He told me that he knew these people socially, which I didn't know because neither of them had mentioned it to me. He said he liked them very much and he found both were talented, both had worked professionally, and he could see them both going back to work again independently without being married. Then it became clear to me that his preconceived attitude about these people, his prejudice about these two people, had prevented him from really looking at the situation. If he had looked as an analyst would look, instead of as a friend would look, if he looked as someone who wants to help and have a patient, or send a patient to someone, he wouldn't have made such peculiar recommendations.

I agree that your motivations certainly influence what motivation you're going to find in your patients. Whether you need a patient or don't need a patient plays a big role in this, so it's very important that you always analyze this in yourself.[75] Is your need or lack of need for a patient obscuring your judgment, or is your liking for these people obscuring your judgment? Many times a friend will consult you or

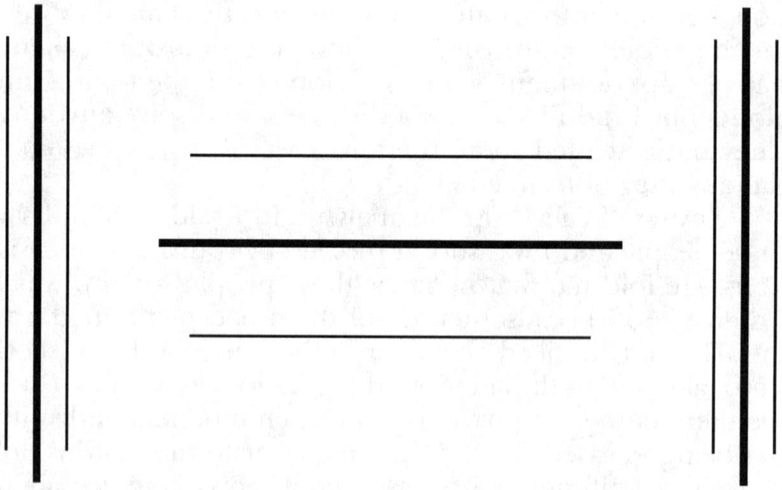

an acquaintance that you like, and the fact that you like them will complicate and obscure your real evaluation of the case. That's why it's so much better not to do it, but sometimes you can't help it. They come as friends, they want to talk with you, you don't know what it's all about, and you can't say no before they pour out a story.

## Ending the Preliminary Interviews

Now, I want to drop this business of motivation and go on. We haven't got this patient into analysis, and we haven't even finished the preliminary interviews. I'm determined to finish it today. Let's talk about this last phase: the ending of the preliminary interviews. Whatever the time interval is, whatever you've allotted for this case, how do you end these interviews? What are the procedures and considerations to keep in mind in ending these interviews? There are certain key factors you must bear in mind, which I will briefly mention and then we will discuss it to see if you agree and what you can add.

### Do Not End the Initial Interviews Abruptly

First of all, above all, never suddenly end a preliminary interview. If you know all you have is one hour's time, and your schedule doesn't allow more, please indicate this to your patient a good enough period in advance of the end of the hour. Say to the patient, well, look we only have another twenty minutes, or half hour to come to our conclusions. If I can tell we will need more time, early or in the middle of the first hour I will ask the patient, will you be able to come back a second time, because I don't think we're going to finish? Do that if you don't think you're going to finish, so that the end is not abrupt. You need to prepare the patient for the end. The amount of time available is worthy of discussion, so say to the patient, look, I'm sorry I don't have any more time, and we have to come to some conclusions

[76] This short section on making the goals of the initial interviews clear to the patient is relevant for all approaches to treating psychological, emotional problems, be they analytic therapies, medications, cognitive–behavioral therapies or others. It is not possible to build a treatment alliance (for Greenson the working alliance), without fully including the patient as a partner to the initial interviews at every step along the way. Patients should not be asked to arbitrarily accept procedures that they are capable of understanding. From the first meeting, the patient should have a sense of what will happen, how long it will take, what the steps will be along the way, and what is reasonable to expect. As Greenson comments in the next section, "nothing is vague, mysterious, or authoritarian."

in this hour, as tentative as they are, so please try to tell me as much as you can. Or, I'll say something like, since this is a rather complicated situation, I think we ought not try to finish this in this hour, will you have time, as I will have time next week to see you for another hour or so?

## Make the Goals of the Initial Interviews Clear[76]

I think the whole question of how much time you have available should be clear and specific. Also, you have to indicate what you will try to do in this amount of time, or what you have tried to do with this amount of time. With some patients I say, all I can do is evaluate if you need treatment and what kind of treatment. Or all I can do is establish, is this an emergency or isn't it, and do we have time? Or all I can do is guide you into the proper channels. Now some patients come with a recommendation. A man came from New York last week and the analyst in New York told him, "Dr. Greenson won't have time to treat you, but he will see that you get into the proper hands." Or in the marital problem that I told you about, I said at the end of a half an hour: Now this is too complicated to solve in one hour, so this hour try to give me a picture of this marriage of yours, and then I will see both of you separately. I want to indicate and outline what I would like to do with the preliminary interviews, because in some cases I won't treat them myself. I think that indicating the limits of the time, the goals, and what I'm trying to do for the patient is very important in the preliminary interviews.

## Give the Patient a Chance to Ask Questions

Also, before I have finished in a given an hour, I always leave enough time to turn to the patient and say, we're going to have to stop in a few minutes, do you have any questions you'd like to ask me? Otherwise at the end of the hour it can be: Oh doctor, by the way I didn't tell you so-and-so.

Then you keep the next patient waiting, and you're worried about the patient waiting. So I allow myself enough time for the patient to ask some questions and to give him the answers.

## Make the Treatment Recommendations Clear

I never take more than three hours for this preliminary interviewing and assessment. Most often it's one hour, because that's all the time I have for appraisals. But whether it be one, two, or three hours, in the final portion I say, here are my conclusions. I like to give my conclusions in very simple, precise, nontechnical terms. I will explain if I do or don't have the time, how much treatment is needed, whether it should be analytical treatment or psychotherapeutic treatment. I talk to patients in general, nontechnical ways. I don't think I am absolute in what I say. I never say you must have analysis. I might say, you ought to be in a hospital, or I feel pretty certain that you should be in a hospital. I also say I may be missing something. I like to leave a little loophole for both of us to find out whatever the appraisal and the recommendations bring up. It happens. Some damned complication comes up like the patient says, incidentally I don't like Los Angeles and I plan to go back to New York.

Now in addition to all of this I feel the patient is entitled to an explanation of the reasons for the recommendation. Let's say I have taken a full three hours for the preliminary interviews and I feel this man ought to be analyzed. I will tell him I think he ought to be analyzed. I'll say, it seems to me this would be the method of choice, and I will explain why, the kind of problem he has needs a very thorough, intensive kind of treatment. I'll explain that it's not enough merely to try to avoid or overcome certain isolated symptoms, that it has invaded major areas, and to get into the causes of this means to go back deeply into this man's past life, because they go back a long time. I'll tell him that the best treatment for achieving this is in analytic therapy. So I

[77] Greenson refers here to authors who have written books for the general public about what psychoanalysis is and how to decide if it is the appropriate treatment (e.g., Horney, 1946). His point here is that such books cannot teach people to know if they need psychoanalysis or any other psychotherapy for that matter. It is necessary to conduct the initial interviews, to formulate an opinion about a person so that they can be helped to understand a treatment recommendation within the context of their own particular problems. Understanding treatment recommendations is part of the overall process of the initial interviews, and it is a part of the process whereby patients come to have a better understanding about themselves.

give a certain amount of explanation as to why I have come to my conclusion, and then I will say, now what do you think about it? I always feel the patient is entitled to ask questions and to understand the reasons for the recommendation. If patients come to see me saying they were recommended for psychotherapy, I say, I'm glad to hear what Dr. so-and-so says, but let me form my own opinion, so please tell me something about you and let's see. I will even say, it's no disrespect to Dr. so-and-so, but I like to form my own opinion.

You know that a surgeon would not open a belly on the diagnosis of someone else, he palpates too, and he takes his own examination, and then he decides. I feel I have exactly the same right to do this because God knows I have been sent some monstrous cases for analysis in my career. Some of these cases were sent by very, so-called well-trained, competent people, who felt they were doing me a favor to boot, and yet to me it's as though they saw another patient.

## How to Explain the Recommendation for Analysis

*Candidate:* I'd like to hear more about how to clarify the treatment recommendations to the patient who is naive about psychoanalysis.

*Greenson:* It may be alien, but I feel it can be explained relatively simply. Let me just give you an example of how I do it. Let's say the man is really pretty naive, or the woman. Now I would say, when I come to my conclusions: Mr. Greenberg, now we've talked two times and I feel on the basis of what you've told me that you need a special kind of therapy. I don't know how familiar you are with psychotherapy or psychoanalysis, do you know what these things are? Now let's say he says: "Well, very vaguely. I once read a book." Usually it will be Karen Horney, Erich Fromm, or Reisman, so they don't know anything about it.[77] Then I will say, now let me briefly explain it to you. It's rather

complicated, and all I can do is give a rather simple explanation, but see if you get the gist of it.

I'll go on to say: There are two major kinds of therapies, ways of treatment, for emotional disturbances, and that's what you have, an emotional disturbance, either in the form of fear or whatever. There are two major ways of treating it. One is to cover up the symptom, to give you some pills, to tell you to go on a vacation, to say forget about it, and to encourage you to run away. In your case, I don't feel this kind of treatment would be the best for you. You need a whole other kind of treatment. The other kind of treatment is to try to uncover, to explore: What makes this man afraid at night, what happened to him in his life, in his experiences? Why is he like this? Now the peculiar part of it is you don't know why. All you know are very superficial and partial answers, because the things that caused it have been forgotten and are no longer in your conscious mind. Therefore our treatment, in order to be helpful, has to find out about all these things. So I say: What you need is an uncovering kind of psychotherapy. Now to complicate matters even more there are two kinds, at least, of uncovering psychotherapies. There is a kind of brief, symptom focused, analytic psychotherapy, and then there is a more intensive, extensive, deeper psychotherapy. The deeper one we call psychoanalysis. The difference is one of depth, and I think the best way we can assure the best results is to go the deepest and longest route.

Now that's sort of roughly the idea. I don't go into how many times we'll meet a week until I get the reactions of the patient to this information, but this is what I explain to a relatively intelligent but uneducated man. With people who are more intelligent, it's easier. Nevertheless I still explain pretty much the same. Do you get the drift of it? I go into so much detail as I told you, and I would be just as systematic as I told you. I want the patient to see already that I'm forthright, direct, concrete, and as exact as I can be. Because that is the analytic atmosphere, it is how I say everything. Nothing vague, mysterious, or authoritarian. I explain the way I think, how it will be done, and why.

[78] Greenson's comments were made at a time when psychoanalysis was a popular treatment approach. It was more common in 1959 to begin with analysis than it is today. Nevertheless, the candidate's comment that "psychotherapy preceding analysis is not always a bad thing" addresses the more common current-day practice of beginning patients in psychotherapy and at some pointing converting the treatment into analysis. Greenson is allowing that analysis does not have to begin "uncontaminated" by prior efforts at psychotherapy. For example, he would not see it as essential that the psychotherapist/psychoanalyst refer the patient to someone else if the patient accepts a recommendation for analysis after a period of psychotherapy. Nowadays, there is significantly less concern on average with the idea that conversion from psychotherapy to psychoanalysis is inherently problematic.

*Candidate:* One problem is the patient who has enough motivation and an analyzable neurosis, but who isn't terribly sick and isn't suffering terribly. Is it really worthwhile for me to do it? Do I really need it? Is it a luxury for me or is it necessary for me?

*Greenson:* My answer to this is usually to say, it depends on you. You might temporarily persuade a patient to go into analysis, only to have that persuasion die down with the first negative transference or the sexual transference. I'd rather have this kind of resistance come up in the beginning, so my answer to the patient who asks if it's worthwhile is to say: I don't know, it depends on you. If you don't feel this is what you want, I would recommend not to do it now. Wait until such a time when you really feel it's indicated. Maybe as time goes on and you see how miserable you are, because of all the things you aren't able to accomplish and enjoy, then you will feel like coming. You see, I'm already giving a suggestion in the direction of maybe tomorrow, but I would not try to persuade a patient. I'm a rather persuasive person and I have talked many people into analysis, only to see soon after that the whole thing wasn't necessary. They felt great. So I'm careful not to be persuasive in that way. I would not push patients into analysis. I find it's tough enough to analyze a patient who is well motivated, even latently well motivated, but those who aren't really motivated, brother!

*Candidate:* I've had cases after several months of psychotherapy who become more motivated for analysis, and these people can do well. On the other hand, I have seen people who jumped into analysis only to fail, so psychotherapy preceding analysis is not always a bad thing.[78]

*Greenson:* I agree with you. Also, you need to be aware that times have changed. It used to be different. Let me tell you, twenty years ago, God knows, you had few analysts who did psychoanalytic psychotherapy. Prior to World War II all the analysts were classically trained analysts who had little if any

[79] This is an interesting passage. It is extremely honest and forthright. Greenson is saying that in 1939 psychoanalysis was recommended more often than it was indicated, in cases where other treatments would have been more appropriate and helpful. This is certainly a central issue for the initial interviews today as much as it was then. How often are recommendations determined more by what the interviewer is trained to provide than by the best interests of the patient? How often today are treatment recommendations determined by the insurance company's reimbursement policies? Certainly these problems demand that psychotherapists be familiar with the indications for a variety of treatment methods, and be willing and able to offer patients options (referrals if necessary) with clear explanations of the advantages and disadvantages of the various options.

[80] It is interesting to note that in 1959 there was a sense that analysts were taking patients into intensive treatment who were more and more disturbed, and this was a topic of discussion that came up frequently in the 1990s. It seems that the trend Greenson notes here has continued in some areas but not in others. For example, with the advent of more effective antipsychotic medications there is less psychoanalytic treatment done with psychotic populations, but with the increase in effective antidepressant medications, more depressed patients are able to participate in exploratory, insight-oriented treatments like psychoanalysis.

psychiatric experience. Most of them were just straight analysts, and they did very little psychoanalytic psychotherapy. It was considered either beneath them or too difficult, usually beneath them, so the patients walked in and in a few minutes they were on the couch. I see a change today in that we are more broadly trained, and we are much more careful in recommending analysis, I think partly because of our bad experiences. Many patients who have been through a course of years of analysis have done poorly; let's face it, it's true. I think many of these patients did not do well because they were selected badly and not given alternatives.[79]

*Candidate:* Although we do try to evaluate our patients much more carefully, I think that we generally have more disturbed patients in intensive treatment today as compared to four years ago.[80]

*Greenson:* This is also true. I do think we're seeing in consultation patients who are sicker. It brings up an interesting question of diagnosis: Is it that patients are sicker or that they were improperly diagnosed before? When I think back to the cases I treated when I was a candidate, I'm sure at least two of them were misdiagnosed by me and my supervisor. Today I would say they were borderline psychotics, but we didn't think so because there were hysterical features in the case, so we called them hysterics with certain unusual things. Now we say, meschuggeh with a touch of hysteria. I think we more frequently recognize when we're dealing with sicker people, in part because we've had bad experiences. This is a main reason why we want to learn more, because we want to be careful. At any rate, this is the point of our depending on the interviews.

# 13 Concluding Remarks

Let me say a few words about the duration of these interviews. First of all, how long I do it depends primarily on the amount of time I have, since I usually keep only one hour a week free for consultations. I do it because I like consultations, and I do it because it's interesting to see new people. Also, I like to refer patients to friends, colleagues, and candidates who need patients. I have a lot of friends all over the country these many years I have practiced, so I like to keep an hour a week open for consultation. Therefore I usually limit the preliminary interviews to one hour, which means a rough assessment, diagnosis, and then a referral.

Let me add something here about the source of information about the patient. I certainly don't want to know anything that the patient doesn't know. I don't want historical data from an outside source that the patient doesn't know, because I don't want to be burdened with having to keep a secret from the patient. I don't mind knowing some clinical data and some clinical formulations that an analyst will make about his patient, but when an analyst will say, "I heard such-and-such from the patient's mother, or the husband told me so and so," I don't want to know it. I find it a nuisance, and I try to discourage learning such information whether I'm analyzing the patient or not.

Let me tell you what I would like to cover next time. Since we have finished the preliminary interviews, we will briefly take up the analyzability of the patient. Then I think we ought to talk about the choice of analyst, how do you decide who would be the analyst? Should you take the patient or not? If you can't take the patient, who do you send them to? Why? If it is a homosexual patient, do you send them to a man or a woman? What makes you decide? How do you pick your referrals, besides the fact that they're your friends and they need patients? Isn't there a difference in the way people work with certain patients? There certainly is. Do you pay attention to your hunches to some extent? Do you want to treat the patient? What about keeping a patient on a waiting list, how do you feel about this? Once we have decided the patient is to be analyzed, I want to talk about the transition to the couch. How do we get the patient onto the couch? Do you discuss the rules of missed hours, smoking, changing the life situations? How? How do you discuss the frequency of hours and the duration of treatment when the patient wants to know how long it will take? How do you discuss the fee? What do you tell the patient about the couch? Finally, do you tell the patient this will be a trial analysis or not? Let's stop here and pick it up next time.

# References

American Psychiatric Association (1968), *Diagnostic and Statistical Manual of Mental Disorders,* 2nd ed. (DSM-II). Washington, DC: American Psychiatric Press.

———— (1994), *Diagnostic and Statistical Manual of Mental Disorders,* 4th ed. (DSM-IV). Washington, DC: American Psychiatric Press.

Appelbaum, S. A. (1977), *The Anatomy of Change: A Menninger Foundation Report on Testing the Effects of Psychotherapy.* New York: Plenum.

Bacon, G. L., Benedek, T., Fuerst, R. A., Gerard, M. W., Alexander, F., French, T. M., et al. (1946), *Psychoanalytic Therapy.* New York: Ronald Press.

Blatt, S. (1974), Object representation in anaclitic, introjective depression. *The Psychoanalytic Study of the Child,* 29:107–157. New Haven, CT: Yale University Press.

DeLeon, P., Ed. (1998), *Professional Psychology: Research and Practice,* 29(1).

Deutsch, F. (1939), The associative anamnesis. *Psychoanal. Quart.,* 8:354.

Freud, S. (1905), Fragment of an analysis of a case of hysteria. *Standard Edition,* 7:3–122. London: Hogarth Press, 1953.

――― (1910), "Wild" psycho-analysis. *Standard Edition,* 11:219–227. London: Hogarth Press, 1957.

――― (1913), On beginning the treatment. *Standard Edition,* 12:121–144. London: Hogarth Press, 1958.

――― (1923), The Ego and the Id. *Standard Edition,* 19:3–66. London: Hogarth Press, 1961.

Gill, M. (1951), Ego psychology and psychotherapy. *Psychoanal. Quart.,* 20:62.

――― (1954), Psychoanalysis and exploratory psychotherapy. *J. Amer. Psychoanal. Assn.,* 2:771–797.

Greenson, D. (1992), Assessment of analyzability. In: *The Technique and Practice of Psychoanalysis,* Vol. 2. *A Memorial Volume to Ralph R. Greenson,* ed. A. Sugarman, R. A. Nemiroff, & D. P. Greenson. New York: International Universities Press.

Greenson, R. (1960), Empathy and its vicissitudes. In: *Explorations in Psychoanalysis.* New York: International Universities Press, 1978, pp. 147–162.

――― (1967), *The Technique and Practice of Psychoanalysis,* Vol. 1. New York: International Universities Press.

――― (1979), Beginnings: The preliminary contacts with the patient. In: *The Technique and Practice of Psychoanalysis,* Vol. 2. *A Memorial Volume to Ralph R. Greenson,* ed. A. Sugarman, R. A. Nemiroff, & D. P. Greenson. New York: International Universities Press.

Horney, K. 1946), *Are You Considering Psychoanalysis?* New York: W. W. Norton.

Kernberg, O. (1975), *Borderline Conditions and Pathological Narcissism.* New York: Jason Aronson.

――― (1984), *Severe Personality Disorders.* New Haven, CT: Yale University Press.

Kissen, M. (1986), *Assessing Object Relations Phenomena.* Madison, CT: International Universities Press.

Knight, R. P. (1953), Borderline states. *Bull. Menninger Clinic,* 17:1–12.

Kwawer, J. S., Lerner, H. D., Lerner, P. M., & Sugarman, A. (1980), *Borderline Phenomena and the Rorschach Test.* New York: International Universities Press.

Lerner, P. M. (1991), *Psychoanalytic Theory and the Rorschach.* Hillsdale, NJ: Analytic Press.

Moraitis, G. (1995), The couch as a protective shield for the analyst. *Psychoanal. Inq.,* 15:406–412.

Rapaport, D., Gill, M., & Schafer, R. (1945–1946), *Diagnostic Psychological Testing,* rev. ed., ed. R. Holt. New York: International Universities Press, 1968.

Reik, T. (1937), *Surprise and the Psychoanalyst.* New York: Dutton.

———— (1948), *Listening with the Third Ear.* New York: Farrar, Straus.

Ross, J. M. (1999), Once more onto the couch: Consciousness and preconscious defenses in psychoanalysis. *J. Amer. Psychoanal. Assn.,* 47(1):91–111.

Schafer, R. (1954), *Psychoanalytic Interpretation in Rorschach Testing.* New York: Grune & Stratton.

———— (1967), *Projective Testing and Psychoanalysis.* New York: International Universities Press.

# Name Index

# Subject Index

211